My Mulligan to Golf

The Hilarious Story of Shell's Wonderful World of Golf &
the Beginning of the Champions Tour

BY FRED RAPHAEL

with

DON WADE

EDITED BY MARTIN DAVIS

The American Golfer

Golfer

My Mulligan to Golf

The Hilarious Story of Shell's Wonderful World of Golf &
the Beginning of the Champions Tour

FIRST EDITION

Published by:
The American Golfer, Inc.
200 Railroad Avenue
Greenwich, Connecticut 06830
(203) 862-9720
FAX: (203) 862-9724
EMAIL: IMD@aol.com
WEBSITE: TheAmericanGolfer.com

ISBN: 1-888-531-15-0
EAN: 978-1-888531-15-2

We wish to thank Terry Galvin and Adam Schupak for their invaluable editorial assistance and Oksanna Babij for her fine art direction. We also wish to acknowledge the editorial assistance of Steve Indiviri, Cori Lantz and Alex Friedman of our staff for their diligence in research and fact checking.

For Bob Rubler, a great guy and a better friend.

PROLOGUE

The story of MY MULLIGAN TO GOLF is actually two stories. The first has to do with my roles as Producer and Director of the *Shell's Wonderful World of Golf* series, beginning in 1960 and ending in 1970, and then with *The Liberty Mutual Legends of Golf,* which started as the germ of an idea back in 1963 while I was still very much involved with the Shell project. *The Legends of Golf* developed into what became the "Sports Success Story of the 1980s" — the Champions Tour. The two stories will always be linked as one for me because the golfers whom I invited to the original *Legends* in 1978 first crossed my path during the Shell series. Without *Shell's Wonderful World of Golf* there would never have been a *Liberty Mutual Legends of Golf* and, in all probability, no Champions Tour.

INTRODUCTION

The original *Shell's Wonderful World of Golf* was a 92-match series of hour-long television programs featuring the world's leading golfers playing the world's most famous and difficult courses in 48 countries on every continent. The series was more than head-to-head competition between two of the game's finest golfers. It was an examination of golf — of the features that made some courses truly great and world famous; of the styles and techniques employed by the leading professionals; of the customs and the atmosphere in which golf is played in far-off countries and, perhaps most important of all, of the "why" of golf.

Many of the courses played in the series could be famous for their beauty alone, but all the courses, each representative of the best in its part of the world, had one thing in common: they were demanding. On any of those courses an innocent-looking shot slightly misplayed could mean almost irretrievable disaster for even the best golfers. And the matches proved to American golf fans that there were many excellent golfers all over the world.

Filming of the series was an odyssey that started at Pine Valley Golf Club in New Jersey and ended nine years later in San Francisco. Our journey covered approximately one million miles and we had at our command more than 50 motion picture, television and golf experts—and enough equipment to fill a large moving van to overflowing.

Our cameras — which filmed every shot played (well almost, but more on that later) — exposed thousands of miles of color film, and recorders used miles of audio tape — all for one purpose: to meticulously capture the play, the character of the courses and the spirit of these great matches and the countries in which they were played.

The Liberty Mutual Legends of Golf originally was conceived as a series of matches between the over-50 greats of the game in a team-play format, much like the old CBS Golf Classic. However, after NBC Sports agreed that the idea had a future on television, we refined it to one "live" event which NBC would televise annually.

These projects consumed almost half of my life. The Shell series ended in 1970 and *The Legends of Golf* finally became a reality in 1977. The intervening years were full of disappointments and rejections. "Who would want to watch a bunch of old men play golf?" was the reaction I often received from the television networks, syndicates and other sources that I tried to enlist in my effort to find a media outlet for my project.

But I was determined to stay with it and in the end my persistence paid off. Over the years I've been asked the same question: Was it worth it? The answer, as with the experience of sinking a winning putt or hitting the occasional perfect drive, is absolutely. As I look back, not only on my Shell days but my last 20 years with *The Legends*, I consider myself a most fortunate man. Thanks to Shell, I traveled all over the world for 10 years. After 20 years with *The Liberty Mutual Legends of Golf*, I can reflect on having given "Mulligans" to my many friends in the game. As the years go on, many other seniors, who probably never knew me, will enjoy their travels and million dollar purses, and I'm thrilled to have played a part in that.

I wish to thank the former President of Shell, Monroe E. Spaght, and also Melvin E. Bradshaw, Chairman of the Board of Liberty Mutual Insurance, who made it all happen for me. I'd also like to thank my dear friend, Gene Sarazen, who over dinner one night at the Masters, just happened to mention that the next day the "Old Legend, Gene Sarazen, was playing with the Future Legend, Arnold Palmer." The word "legend" stayed with me and became the seed for *MY MULLIGAN TO GOLF.*

Shell's Wonderful World of Golf

1961 – 1970

CHAPTER 1

When Shell first conceived the idea of presenting international golf in a network television series, it never imagined that at its completion, nine years later, we would have filmed and televised 92 one-hour matches in 48 countries and on every continent.

Shell eventually found itself in the unique position of owning an Emmy-award television production as well as the world's longest running and widest-viewed golf program. It was estimated that the programs attracted a weekly audience of from 10 million to 12 million people. We won an Emmy award in 1966 and were nominated for a second Emmy in 1967. The series premiered in 1962 on CBS and lasted throughout 1970 (and was reborn again in 1994).

The show began inauspiciously on an overcast Monday morning in June 1961. The location of this inaugural match was the world-famous Pine Valley Club in Clementon, New Jersey. Two legends of the game, Byron Nelson and Gene Littler, were competing in our first *Shell's Wonderful World of Golf* match.

Byron won the toss and hit his drive down the center of the fairway. You can imagine my shock when one of my cameramen came down from his tower, on the first fairway, ran out to the ball, picked it up, threw it back to the first tee and over his walkie talkie shouted, "Fred, have him hit it again. I missed it!"

If you ever run across someone who tells you that he saw the first shot ever filmed in the series, don't believe it. We never caught it on film. But we did catch every other one.

From that rather auspicious start, *Shell's Wonderful World of Golf* aired on all three major networks from 1962 until 1970.

Video techniques, such as instant replay, slow motion and split screens, which today are a regular part of any sports event, were unique and rarely seen when we began. I believe that the slow motion, freeze- frame and split-screen techniques which we employed, beginning with the very first show, were the first times such techniques were used in golf telecasts.

It's amazing what you can do with ingenuity and hard work.

The Shell series was my introduction to the game of golf. Prior to my involvement with the project, I had never played the game, never watched it on television, never followed it in the press and had never stepped foot on a golf course.

How did I get into it? Well, I guess I just happened to be in the right place at the right time. For 12 years I had been with the J. Walter Thompson Advertising Agency, running its Television Commercial Production Department. In 1958, I decided to change careers, moving to the independent television world as a producer.

While I was in the midst of making this transition, something that I was not a part of was happening in Westchester County, New York, that would change my professional career forever. It was a conversation at the Sleepy Hollow Country Club in Scarborough-on-Hudson, between Mr. Monroe E. Spaght, President of the Shell Oil Company; Gordon Biggar, Vice President of Public Relations at Shell, and Vic Armstrong, Senior Vice President of the Kenyon & Eckhardt Advertising Agency. K & E handled the public relations for Shell and Ogilvy & Mather ran the advertising and marketing end of the business.

They had just completed a round of golf and were having a drink when the conversation turned to golf on television. It wasn't at all strange that talk was about golf and television because at that moment a program called "All Star Golf" was on the club-house television. After a few minutes, Mr. Spaght said he wished someone could put together a show for Shell — one that would be different, spectacular, well-produced and do justice to the game of golf. And then he asked, "Why don't we just do it?"

Now, as we all know, these things are said all the time when high-powered executives meet after a round of golf — especially after a few pops — but for the most part, nothing ever comes of them. However, this was not the case because when Mr. Spaght wanted something done, he was not one to let go of an idea. And when he said he wanted a golf show to be the finest ever produced, he meant just that. It was his belief in his "Pursuit of Excellence" that encouraged us to never cut corners and to produce only the best program that we could deliver.

About a month or so went by and nothing happened. Then at a staff meeting one morning, Mr. Spaght asked what was happening with his suggestion. Nothing had been done, Biggar confessed, but when Gordon got back to his office, telephones began ringing off the hook. As a result, the Shell series and my new career were just beginning to unfold...and I still knew nothing about it. The year was 1961 and I was working for a commercial production company, Filmways. My boss was a man named Marty Ransohoff, a low-handicap golfer. I remember it was a Thursday and Marty had been off to a meeting at K & E with the Shell folks. I had no idea of what the meeting was about.

When Marty returned, he came into my office and asked me what my handicap was. I was totally confused. I had no idea what he was talking about. He could tell by the twisted expression on my face that I was puzzled by his question. He repeated it, and I finally asked him what in the hell he was talking about. Your "golf handicap," he said. I laughed and told him that golf was a totally foreign game to me. He shook his head, turned and left my office. He later explained that Shell was interested in producing a golf project and they were looking for new ideas for presenting the game on television. Marty told me to give it some thought but not to spend too much time with it because "it will really never fly."

Well, it *would* fly, in fact it would soar, because Mr. Spaght had played golf all over the world and he wanted to bring international golf — and especially championship golf courses — to the attention of the American golfing public. With Marty's reluctant and skeptical go-ahead, I began my education in the world of golf.

My first step was to call my contacts at Shell and ask for any information they might have on the history of the company. After a short walk to 30 Rockefeller Plaza, I began to immerse myself in the history of Shell and the entire Royal Dutch Shell family.

Next, I visited the New York City Public Library, one of the world's great libraries, and spent two days educating myself on the history and the "why and how" of the game of golf. I believe I went through about eight or nine books, most of them written by one of golf's leading authorities, Herbert Warren Wind, who was then the golf editor at *Sports Illustrated* and who would later move to *The New Yorker*.

As a result of this rapid education, I realized that Shell and golf had at least one thing in common: They were both very active around the world. Hence my presentation became "Around the World with Golf and Shell." I did not have the title right yet, but I was warming to the idea.

I believe my best contribution to the format and to our cause at Filmways was when I walked into a meeting at K & E with the largest map of the world I could find. Using small photos of 707 aircraft, and using orange and blue pins to point out the cities where we might play, I believe I caught their attention. And, I believe as they gazed at that map, for the first time, they realized the magnitude of the project someone was going to undertake on their behalf.

My presentation included the fact that while at JWT, the agency came up with a campaign fashioned after a popular movie of that time, *Around the World in 80 Days*. In the campaign for the Ford Motor Company, our production company, Filmways, took Ford cars around the world in just 80 days. Anyway, our experience at Filmways with this unusual project helped give us an advantage over our competition and helped us walk off with an agreement to produce the golf series for Shell.

We now had the contract and I had the title of "Executive Producer." I have always taken great pride in being fortunate and smart enough to surround myself with the best people in the trade, so, with Ransohoff's help, we hired an excellent director from Hollywood, Dick Darley, who also knew absolutely nothing about golf. Since there was to be a considerable amount of aerial photography, we hired Tom Tutwiller, who had been the Director of Photography on the "Spirit of St. Louis," a movie about Charles Lindbergh starring Jimmy Stewart. What we did not know at the time we hired "Tut" was that he never actually went up in a plane to do any of the aerial photography for the film — and he wasn't about to start with our series. Realizing that the editing of this series, which was to consist of 11 one-hour programs (the other two hours of this 13-week series were going to feature Leonard Bernstein concerts) would be a long and tedious affair, we hired one of the finest editors in New York City, Sy Singer, as our supervising editor. Sy went about the business of hiring the best staff available. What was strange — even eerie — about all this hiring was the fact that no one knew anything about the game of golf.

In a way, having a nucleus of a crew who had no knowledge of the game turned out to be a blessing in disguise. For example, when our luggage was passing through customs, you never saw a golf bag. We were going around the world to work, not play golf. And, we eventually did put together a winning team…and, yes, in the latter years a few golf bags did become part of our luggage. Many of us became hopelessly hooked on the game.

One early member in our permanent party was our announcer,

George Rogers. George came out of Baltimore and was a Mack Edwards contribution. George and I became sociable drinking buddies and spent many a night closing "Kenny's Pub" in New York City, occasionally listening to Sammy Cahn, the famous writer of many popular hits.

George was a talented announcer but he could be testy when things didn't go his way. I didn't play much golf, but when I did play, I always tried to play with George. You see, George was the kind of golfer who insisted he was a 10-handicap player. But he rarely broke 100, at least when he played with me, so I let his ego claim that he was a 10 and, since I was a legitimate 30, he usually bought the beers.

At least with George I finally had a member of the crew who had considerable golf knowledge and he would stay on in New York to work with our editing team. Edna Forde, our script girl from Dublin, Ireland, also was an important spoke in the wheel when it came to accomplishing the monumental task of editing the enormous amount of film footage. Edna had recorded — and remembered — every shot and her work was irreplaceable in the cutting room.

I believe that it was around the third year in the series that I hired Al Barkow to join our staff. Al was a writer and I hired him to work on scripts with Rogers. I met Al through a friend, Mary Ann Donohue. She had left JWT and was working at McGraw-Hill when she met Al. Somehow, my name came up during a conversation with Barkow, who was also at McGraw-Hill writing "How to" books for the company.

Al was an excellent golfer and she arranged for Al and me to get together at Costello's, a celebrated East Side watering hole, for a few beers one evening. Al enjoyed listening to all of my *Shell's Wonderful World of Golf* stories and I hired Al to join our crew. By the time Al left the program six years later, he had become my Associate Producer/Writer. He then went on to become editor of *Golf* Magazine and, later, *Golf Illustrated.*

By now, I had held a number of meetings with my friends at Shell and the agency, and the dreaded moment of truth was at hand. They asked me to join them in a round of golf at Pine Valley. How could I refuse? I wish I could have thought of a way.

Gene Sarazen, who was our expert analyst, had outfitted me with a set of new Wilson clubs and when he heard I was playing with my new-found friends, he offered me six dozen golf balls. We Italians stick together.

Well, we completed our round and no one at Shell could ever accuse me of lying to them about my golf experience. I believe my score for the day was 154. When I think back and come to the realization that my first round of golf was at Pine Valley, I should have realized that my friends were sadists at heart. I still shudder when I remember it.

About a month later, one of our foursome called me to his office and proceeded to read a letter he and other members of Pine Valley had received from Pine Valley's president, the formidable Mr. J. Arthur Brown. In it, Mr. Brown announced that his grounds crew had found as many as 29 British-size golf balls — which were illegal in the United States — and that if he found the culprit, he would be tossed out of the club, never to return. He asked if I had any comment.

"Tell Mr. Brown to keep looking," I said, "there are four more still out there."

That was my introduction to actually playing the game of golf. I can thank Sarazen, who had given me the clubs and balls. He never offered more and I never asked for any. About that time, it turned out that I was not the only one who knew we were assembling a team of non-golfers. K & E and Shell caught on and before I knew it they had hired Herbert Warren Ward to work with us. To tell you the truth, having Herb around on a daily basis was not easy for either him or our staff. Herb was Yale through and through, and epitomized the atmosphere that surrounds the finest golf clubs in the world.

We were in the film business, not the golf business, but Herb adjusted to us and we to him. I personally had the greatest respect for Herb as both a great writer and a friend. His stories about the game and the personalities who were part of it fascinated me, and my memories of our time together still do. I truly became a Herb Wind fan and he gave me a knowledge of the history of golf that I never appreciated before.

Along with Herb came Joseph C. Dey, then the Executive Director of the United States Golf Association and the final word on the Rules of Golf. I was rapidly gaining tremendous respect for Shell. They knew the areas where I needed help and they went all out to protect me. From Joe, I learned about the integrity of the game. A quiet gentleman, Joe attended just about every one of our screening sessions. We always had a first screening where everyone took turns at tearing our first rough cut of the show apart and then a second screening to see if we were awake and paying attention at the first session. If, for any reason, Joe missed a session, he would send over his second-in-command, another very highly respected golf authority from the USGA, P. J. Boatwright. A few years ago, when both Joe and P. J. passed away in such a close span of time, I remember asking Barkow, "Who's watching the integrity of the game?"

I didn't need to worry. The game was — and remains — in good hands.

So I learned about the history of the game from Herb and about the integrity of the game from Joe. I could not have had two better teachers. Between them they gave the Shell Series immediate class and credibility. As for our on-air talent, Herb suggested — and Shell agreed — to hire Gene Sarazen — the "Squire" — and the first man to win the modern professional Grand Slam — the Masters, British Open, U.S. Open and the PGA Championship. Gene was around 59-years-old and could still play a fine round of golf. In fact, in our first year, he and former British Open champion Henry Cotton competed in our match at the famous Old Course at St. Andrews. Although Gene had never had any television experience, he handled himself quite well that first year. In 1965, he wore his Masters green jacket at a match we filmed in Killarney, Ireland. Shortly after that he was advised — in no uncertain terms — by Cliff Roberts, the autocratic chairman of Augusta National, that the jacket was to be worn only at the club during the Masters.

To assist Herb with the writing we hired Len Heidman — another non-golfer. Len was perfect because he was a very well-organized television and film writer and, as a result, was most helpful in developing the format that proved so successful for the series.

We had one more writer — Mack Edwards. Over the nine years, Mack and I developed a great friendship, but Mack could be difficult to deal with at times. Mack worked for K & E and was responsible for the writing and production of the commercials and the travelogues, which were excellent. In fact, no less a figure than Red Smith, the Pulitzer Prize winning columnist for *The New York Times*, said he watched the shows just to see the travelogues. Actually, the idea of the travelogue came from the Filmways personnel. But the travelogues, which usually ran about two minutes, set up the location where we were filming, its customs and the flavor of the country and its people. They set the tone for the match that was to follow.

In addition, another popular feature was our "Tips and Techniques," taken from the professionals who participated in our matches. In most shows we had two players, adding up to approximately 150 clinics. Occasionally these tips caused us some anxious moments.

For example, at The Country Club in Brookline, Massachusetts, we had asked Billy Casper, one of golf's greatest putters, to give our viewers a tip on sinking six-foot putts. As luck would have it, on the 18th hole of our match, Billy was faced with a six-footer to tie Doug Sanders. As he lined up his putt, Sarazen looked at me and asked, "What do we do for our clinic if Billy misses this one?" I told Gene we would have to think up another topic — and fast. We filmed the clinics immediately after the completion of the match, and there was no way I could have

Billy miss a six-footer and then come right back on camera and have him give our viewers a lesson on that very same putt. Much to our relief, Billy made the putt.

In addition to all this — the matches, travelogues, clinics, etc. — Shell annually offered our viewers very colorful booklets on our travels and the matches, but actually getting these booklets was not easy. To get one, you had to go into your local Shell dealer and ask for a card on which you had to write your name and address and then mail it to a post office box. Eventually, you got your book. Over the years, Shell distributed millions of these booklets all over the United States and around the world.

Sarazen, Edwards and myself were the only members of the original cast that lasted throughout the entire series. During that time period, Shell changed presidents three times, as did K & E. We had three new Directors of Public Relations at Shell and four different bosses at the agency. But Gene, Mack and I just kept rolling along, like Old Man River. In fact, speaking of changes, it is interesting that in my more than 30 years in the golf world, I had only two sponsors — the Shell Oil Company and the Liberty Mutual Insurance Company and I was associated with only two projects: *Shell's Wonderful World of Golf* and *The Liberty Mutual Legends of Golf.* So, you might say that I dealt with Wonderful Legends all this time and, yes, at times I did get the feeling that I must be doing something right.

At the completion of the series, our passports would have made an interesting television commercial for a credit card company. Over nine years, our crews visited 46 locations, including Argentina, Australia, the Bahamas, Belgium, Bermuda, Brazil, Canada, Chile,

Colombia, England, France, Germany, Guatemala, Greece, India, Hong Kong, Holland, Ireland, Japan, Jamaica, Kenya, Luxembourg, Malaysia, Mexico, Monaco, Norway, New Zealand, Panama, Philippines, Portugal, Puerto Rico, Scotland, Singapore, Spain, Sweden, Switzerland, Thailand, Virgin Islands, West Indies, Tobago, Wales, Venezuela and, of course, the United States.

As I said earlier, the "star" of this unique program proved to be the most challenging golf courses we could find around the world. Identifying these courses was most interesting. In the first year, Herb Wind had much to do with the selection of courses. Since Herb left after the first year, the responsibility was left up to our committee, which included Joe Dey. A group of us would visit with the Public Relations Director of Shell in London, a fine Irishman named John Drummond. John would direct us to the countries that Shell would prefer to have us visit that year. We would then contact the local Shell country director and he in turn would put us in touch with knowledgeable, local golf authorities in each country. When we arrived for our pre-production sessions, our group would visit each course and then come up with our recommendation.

After the few first years, the countries we visited were determined in discussion between Shell's New York and London offices. The London office was in better position to suggest where we should visit, but for the first year — and since we had no idea as to whether the project would be a success — it was decided that we would play one match in Canada and the other 10 at what we considered the most interesting and challenging courses around the world.

The 11 locations selected for the first year were:
    Banff Springs Golf Course, Canada
    The Old Course at St. Andrews, Scotland
    Kasumigaseki Country Club, Japan
    Pine Valley Golf Club, New Jersey
    Royal Melbourne Golf Club, Australia
    Olgiata Golf Club, Italy
    St. Cloud Golf Club, France
    The Jockey Club, Argentina
    Royal Hong Kong Golf Club, Hong Kong
    Gavea Golf and Country Club, Brazil
    Wentworth Golf Club, England

Our initial selection committee — which was comprised of Herb Wind, Gordon Biggar and Vic Armstrong (with final approval of Mr. Spaght) — certainly did a remarkable job of selecting 11 of the finest and most challenging golf courses around the world.

I was not on that committee and had little input into the final selection of the sites. I am sure if I had the final decision, I probably would have passed on St. Andrews. What kind of golf course has no trees? But then, Sam Snead was not impressed with the Old Course when he first saw it and, according to Herb, Bobby Jones initially thought it was the worst course he ever saw. Oddly enough, some 40 years later, Jones said that if he were limited to choosing one and only one course to play he would, without question, select St. Andrews. Go figure. But at least I was in good company when I reported back to Shell that I was

14

not all that impressed with what I later learned was the most famous course in golf.

It was agreed that the first Shell show would be played at Pine Valley. The club was private and presided over then by Mr. Brown, an autocratic Philadelphia lawyer who ran the club the way he wanted to and the hell with anyone else. What I am trying to say is that you did not just walk onto Pine Valley and think you were going to shoot some film without Brown's blessing. The assignment of getting his approval was turned over to me. My lack of knowledge of the game, and in particular such a great course as Pine Valley, was obvious when I arrived on the course — which is in the middle of nowhere — looked the place over, and thought to myself, this has got to be some kind of joke. All I could see from many of the tees was sand, water and eventually some very small fairways. Joining me was a director at Filmways, Lee Goodman, who also knew nothing about the game but, like myself, Lee was a good salesman and it was our job to sell Mr. Brown. We went around the course with him and Lee kept reassuring Brown about what a great place this course was to film and how proud he and the members at Pine Valley would be when they finally got to see the program on television — and in color. After spending the entire day at Pine Valley, Mr. Brown finally gave his approval provided it could be done in two days, filmed in color, and only if Goodman was the director. We had to schedule our shooting for a Monday and a Tuesday and could not bring our crew in until all play had been finished on Sunday, after 5 p.m. It sounded like an impossible assignment, but Shell wanted Pine Valley on the schedule, so we had to find a way to do it. As for Goodman, my non-golfing director, he did one hell of a job of selling Mr. Brown.

We left Pine Valley, sped back to New York City, which was about two hours away, and then I headed right to the office to see Ransohoff. I told Marty that we had permission to film the show but that we had a lot of problems, starting with our own director. I told Marty that this Mr. Brown of Pine Valley insisted that Lee be the director and as Marty realized, Lee knew nothing about golf. Marty sat there looking at me for a while, then said, "Teach Him!" Talk about the blind leading the blind!

Before the filming took place, I set up a luncheon meeting with Lee and Herb Wind so that Herb might give Goodman some ideas — or better yet, help Herb understand what Lee had in mind for filming this match. Goodman began by diagramming how he wanted to place the cameras around the first hole. As he went on, he explained that this was how he handled a recent filming with Sam Snead. Hearing this, Herb began to feel better about Lee and the project. Still, he was curious about where and when he had filmed Sam. Finally, he asked, "Tell me Lee, where was this match with Snead played?"

A very surprised Goodman looked at Herb and said, "What do you mean match? It was an Alka Seltzer commercial!"

So there we were at Pine Valley with Gene Littler and Byron Nelson. We had a producer, me, a director and a crew that was visiting a golf course for the first time. Fortunately, we did have several knowledgeable men on hand such as Sarazen, who would do the commentary, Wind — and, of course, Rogers, our announcer.

To say that I had an uneasy feeling about what might happen that day would be an understatement. It didn't help matters when some of our clients from Shell and Kenyon & Eckart appeared in our gallery wearing horrible shorts, their bellies sticking out over their belts, and sporting awful looking hats. I guess they never realized they'd be caught on camera (or maybe they did, which is even scarier). Believe me, they were never caught that way again. From that moment on, whenever they appeared at a filming, you just knew that their first stop prior to the golf course was the pro shop or Brooks Brothers.

Nelson had the honor on the first hole and, as I described earlier, hit his drive down the left side of the fairway, opening up the green to his approach shot. As Nelson picked up his tee and walked off, our cameraman came down from his position on the tower and ran to the ball. He picked it up and threw it back toward the first tee and said over his walkie-talkie radio, "Ask him to hit it again, we missed it."

That was the first shot ever played on *Shell's Wonderful World of Golf*!

Over the years, I occasionally questioned myself and wondered if all this really happened. After all, it was a hell of a story. But then, in 1992, at Sarazen's 90th birthday party, I ran into Herb Wind. As we reminisced about the old Shell days, Herb said, "Fred, will you ever forget that opening shot at Pine Valley?" I can't tell you how comforting it was to hear Herb relate the story because for years I thought my mind was playing tricks on me.

There were other mistakes made that day by our inexperienced crew. For example, because the camera crew could not follow the ball, something had to be done. The only solution was to go back to Pine Valley days later and shoot some additional footage. We persuaded Leo Fraser, then professional and owner of the Atlantic City Country Club, to come along with us and hit shots while we filmed the ball rolling along the fairway.

Somehow this got back to the *New York World Telegram*'s old sports columnist, Joe Williams, who was extremely popular in those days. His column almost brought the project to an end before we had started filming in Europe. To read Joe Williams' column you would have thought that we were doing something that was unfair, illegal and unethical. In an attempt to explain our actions, we immediately produced a film which described to the audience — and Mr. Williams in particular — what our technical problems were and that we were not trying to deceive the public. Williams and CBS viewed the film and said that they understood our problems. We included this edited film into our second show the following week and the controversy subsided.

From Pine Valley our crew left for JFK airport for our first visit to Europe. Our 15-member crew arrived at the St. Cloud Golf Club about an hour outside of Paris — or, as Wind said, "20 minutes away if you go out there by way of a French taxi driver."

The caddies at St. Cloud were something else. They were all older and very heavy ladies whom Herb said "would not have been entered into a Miss America contest and they had caddied so long that only a brilliant shot as much as caught their attention."

In Paris, we hired the rest of our film crew and immediately ran into a different set of problems, mostly concerning language. In this match, between the winner of the 1960 PGA Championship, Jay Hebert, and the Belgian national champion, Flory Van Donck, following the ball from tee to green continued to plague us.

We would ask one of our French cameramen, "Did you follow the ball?" and he would smile and say "Oui." Then we would ask, "Did you miss the ball in flight?" He would smile and say "Oui!"

As they say around Paris, "Sacre Bleu!"

In our first year we had other problems. For example, the first match we played in Canada was at the Banff Springs Golf Course, one of the most beautiful courses in the world. It was so beautiful that it could be distracting for the average golfer. The match was scheduled in the middle of September. Anyone familiar with the weather in that part of Canada at that time of the year knows that you could face either beautiful fall weather — or a snowstorm.

Well, we got a terrible snowstorm. Just ask former Masters and PGA champion Jackie Burke Jr. Jackie played Canada's Stan Leonard and it took them almost five days to complete the match. On some days they would be able to play no more than a hole or two. On one occasion our director asked Burke to mark his two-foot putt because the snow was falling so hard. Anyone who knows Jackie can just imagine his reaction when he was told he could come back the next day to sink his putt and continue with the round. "No way," screamed Burke.

And, so the putt became another shot we never recorded officially on film. It was filmed but all we saw on the screen was an image of Jackie putting in the snow.

We also had weather problems at Japan's Kasumigaseki Country Club. Dow Finsterwald was scheduled to play Pete Nakumura but we ran into a monsoon. Dow was scheduled to play in England in the Ryder Cup Matches, so we flew in Bob Rosburg as his replacement.

On this trip we also learned that the Japanese take their golf very seriously. So as not to inconvenience the club members, we usually scheduled our matches early in the week. But because of the monsoon at Kasumigaseki, we had to reschedule our filming for later in the week. I had Herb Wind approach George Mizota, a prominent member of the club and the man who had arranged for us to play at Kasumigaseki, to see if we could play our match over the weekend.

"Oh, no, Mr. Wind, you can't do that," Mr. Mizota said. "We have our red and white matches this weekend. People are coming from all over the four islands and we cannot postpone it."

"You don't understand, Mr. Mizota," said Herb. "This is a very expensive project. We have to do this as soon as we possibly can. Besides we have other commitments around the world. Can't you postpone your club match?"

"You don't understand, Mr. Wind," said Mizota "Our members will be coming from all over Japan. This is the one weekend of the year when we are all together. It cannot be postponed." Despite Herb's intervention, the members had their tournament and our match was delayed for a few more days.

Our match at St. Andrews was played under typically raw, rainy and windy weather, which played havoc with our two contestants — host Gene Sarazan and former British Open champion Henry Cotton, both about age 60.

At one point, after a long delay, George Rogers asked Cotton which club he would hit from one of the fairways.

"Damned if I know" replied Henry, studying the wind. "I knew when I first got here, but now I'll have to re-think it all over again."

If the selection committee had a "Mulligan," I believe they would have passed on the Olgiata Golf Club in Italy. Back then it was just about a year old and on television it looked it! Today, Olgiata is a fine test — but then — oh well, VIVA ROMA! The match did give us an opportunity to produce a fascinating travelogue, which proved to be a winner for the Italian tourist industry.

We found our way "Down Under" to Australia and visited the Royal Melbourne Golf Club for a match between Gary Player and five-time British Open champion Peter Thomson. The course, according to Wind, was one of the best-bunkered courses in the world. We also visited Argentina, where Roberto De Vicenzo played Mike Souchak at the Jockey Club in Buenos Aires, and finally we brought our travels to an end with a match between Mario Gonzalez and Billy Casper in Brazil at the Gavea Golf and Country Club.

Occasionally, we picked a course because of Shell's activity in the country, while at other times the beauty of the country had more than a little something to do with it.

Two that come to mind included the Monte Carlo Golf Club in Monaco and Thailand's Royal Bangkok Sports Club. The Monte Carlo Golf Club was an unusual design located 2,700 feet up in the Alpes-Maratimes mountains. It was short —

around 5,000 yards — and played to a par 66 with eight par 3s. On many of the holes, as the local saying went, if you hit a shot over the green it could easily wind up down the mountain and on the road to Nice. Back in 1910, when this course opened, people used to come up the mountains by horse and carriage. It was a trip of about three hours, which, by the way, included a stop for lunch. But the trip was absolutely beautiful since it included views of Monaco and the Mediterranean. When the fog rolled in, you got an eerie feeling as it settled below you. It was a similar feeling one gets when you're flying in a plane and you break through the clouds. Often, you played in perfectly clear skies with the clouds below you.

What I will always remember most about this match was reaching the sixth hole and seeing a Volkswagen motor down the fairway. As it reached us, it came to a halt and out stepped one of the most beautiful women I had ever seen — Princess Grace of Monaco — our Grace Kelly from Philadelphia and Hollywood.

She was introduced to just about everyone in the crew and even remembered one of our cameramen from her movie days. At one point, she motioned me to her side and wondered how I was going to edit the last three holes because all seven cameras were filming her and not the match between our contestants, Barbara Romack and Ialsa Goldschmidt, a top European amateur. She was close to the truth. When we started to edit the film, we realized that on the three holes she referred to, only one or two cameras were following the players. The rest — and I can't say I blame them — were following Princess Grace's every move.

Thailand's Royal Bangkok Sports Club was constructed

inside a racetrack and bordered cricket and field hockey grounds. The par-66 course had, like the Monaco course, eight par 3s. On every hole, 20-foot-wide "Klongs," or canals, came into play. It wasn't unusual to see a young Thai caddie wading deep into a Klong, looking for a lost ball. One youngster came up with a ball and handed it to Jimmy Demaret.

"Hey look, it's Bob Hope's ball," Jimmy said. "It's got his autograph on it."

There are three seasons in Thailand: Hot, rainy and cool and on the day we played our match with the LPGA's Kathy Whitworth, Carol Mann and Sandra Haynie, it was hot and rainy — extremely hot and rainy.

The women traveled half-way around the world to get to Thailand and had tons of luggage with them. But when I asked what they would wear on match day, they all came with clothes of similar colors. We worked out Sandra's and Kathy's wardrobe, but I had to take Carol downtown to get a blouse for her. Now, as you might know, Carol is 6-feet 3-inches tall and in case you don't know, most Thai women are less than five feet tall. Well, you should have heard the giggling going on in the shops when we asked them to create a blouse for a woman that tall. I believe we finally found a man's shirt in the pro shop for Carol and she and I laughed about it decades later.

At the Real Club de Golf "El Prat," a par-72 layout in Portugal, we witnessed some excellent competition between Frank Beard and Sebastian "Duke" Miguel of Madrid, winner of the Spanish, Portuguese and Peruvian Opens.

This was one of the years that Shell paid $10,000 to anyone

who made a hole-in-one. Shell initiated the offer two years prior to this show, but no one had made an ace. In fact, this was the only one in the entire series. It came on the 10th hole, where Miguel made an ace and Beard had a birdie two. On this one hole, we filmed a total of three strokes. But just to show you what a funny game golf is, on the next hole, Beard's drive landed in a tree and stayed up there for an unplayable lie. We had gone from the best golf to possibly the worst in just two holes.

On the day of the match, I was told that Beard and Miguel had agreed to split the purse of $10,000. I found it difficult to believe that Frank had agreed to split a purse against a golfer he should beat playing left-handed. But "Duke" did not have to split the $10,000 bonus for making an ace with Beard. Sebastian, who lived down the street from the club, walked home with $15,000 while Frank had to fly thousands of miles for only $5,000, despite winning the match.

In Portugal, since the bank was a considerable distance from the club, we had exchanged United States dollars for Portuguese Esquados so when we left the bank we had $25,000 in local currency in our accountant's attaché case. Along the way to the club we were stopped at a police roadblock. Every car was being searched by a horde of policemen looking for thieves who had just robbed a local bank for approximately $1 million dollars. We were naturally worried. When the time came for our car to be searched, we were ordered to step out of the car. Jimmy Demaret took the attaché case filled with money. The police carefully examined our luggage and had us remove all of our clothing. Finally satisfied, they sent us on our way. They never bothered to look at the attaché case.

"If they had looked and found the money, we might still be in jail," Jimmy said later.

An incident took place in Portugal that will give you an idea why Demaret's sense of humor became such an important part of the show. Jimmy always found wonderful, warm ways to needle Gene and, of course, Gene was always trying to find ways to get in a jab or two at Jimmy. Now, I never could find the man who was quicker than Jimmy, so whenever we would come up with something for Gene to toss back to Jimmy, we did. A great deal of Portugal is farm country, so I suggested to Gene that Jimmy, being a city boy from Houston, might come up with a comment or two about being in Portuguese farm country. This dialogue took place between Gene and Jimmy on the first green at the Penina Golf Club during the match between Peter Alliss and Doug Sanders:

Sarazen: "You know, Jimmy, we're here in farm country in Southern Portugal."

Demaret: "Yes, Gene, I know we're in farm country. It's lovely isn't it?"

Sarazen: "It sure is. How would you know this is farm country Jimmy, you're a city boy from Houston?"

Demaret: "Well Gene, it's easy. Why, right over there beyond the fairways used to be rice fields."

Sarazen: "Yes, but do you know that those are almond trees just beyond this green?"

Demaret: "Of course I know they are almond trees, Gene. Just look at the way their nuts are hanging!"

At that point my sound engineer exploded with laughter and

I knew that we had another clip for our blooper reel since nothing like that could go on-air in those far more restrained days.

At one point during our stay in Barcelona the local Shell representative arranged a private audience for Sarazen, Demaret and myself with the Cardinal of Barcelona, a city well known for its many beautiful churches.

We couldn't figure out why we were so blessed — so to speak — but we happily went along. When we were introduced to the Cardinal he gave us a blessing with the Sign of the Cross. He looked at Gene and said, "In the name of the Father," and then at me, "and the son," and finally he turned to Jimmy and said, "and the Holy Spirit."

Boy, the Cardinal had that right!

The Shell Series even occasionally found itself involved in international politics.

Sarazen had not played competitively in several years, so generations of golfers had grown up never having seen him play. But Gene was a bona fide legend and during his playing days he traveled internationally, so wherever we went Gene was usually greeted like a returning hero. Our schedule called for visits to the Far East and when we were in Manila, Sarazen received a telephone call from Shell's New York office asking that when filming ended in Kuala Lumpur, he travel to Rangoon, Burma, before heading to our next scheduled location, Greece. The President of Burma was an avid golfer and he wanted to play with Gene. Because of political differences between Burma and the United States, no American officials had been invited to that country for three years. At first, Sarazen refused to go, but he soon received another call, this time from the Secretary of State, Dean Rusk, urging Sarazen to go to Burma. Gene could be famously stubborn, but I reasoned with him and finally we agreed that if he would go, both George Rogers and I would go with him.

Gene's visa had already been arranged so the Burmese consulate had to work on visas for George and myself — and it sure took some work as well as behind-the-scenes plotting by the Burmese officials to pull it off — as George and I were to discover once we arrived in Burma. When we landed, we were met by about 20 government and club officials. It was stifling hot when we exited the plane at the end of the runway and were taken by bus to the terminal. In an upstairs lounge, we were seated around a table, and while the local dignitaries saluted Gene and toasted him with warm beer, George and I began to wonder what we were doing in Rangoon when we could be in Athens enjoying three days of rest and recreation. We also had lots of company because the local Burmese officials were wondering who we were and why we were there.

After the toasts were completed, Gene acknowledged their welcome and said, "I understand we are the first Americans to have been invited to your country in three years." They nodded in agreement.

"What the hell is the matter with you? Are you all a bunch of Communists?" he said, perhaps feeling the result of a couple drinks on the flight and a few tepid beers.

Welcome to Burma!

The next day, Gene played a round of golf with the captain of the Rangoon Golf Club and George and I played behind them. Tired and hung over, we played mostly in the rough. But we came to our senses when the group playing behind us killed a viper, reportedly one of the deadliest of all snakes, in the rough we had just left. That was enough golf for us during that visit.

The following day, because of the brutal heat and humidity, Gene played with a general and the president at 6 a.m. George and I were having coffee on the club veranda when we were approached by someone from the American Embassy telling us we had to leave the country immediately because we had been issued illegal visas and we had to leave or risk being arrested. When we arrived at the airport there was a problem with our visas, and since the flight to Athens was preparing to leave, it was suggested that we leave our luggage, passports and money and that it would be sent with Sarazen the next day. Sarazen, unaware of what had actually happened, was furious when he arrived in Greece and accused us of having stranded him in Burma. He eventually calmed down and we played a round of golf at the Glyfada Golf Club, trading horror stories from Burma.

Later in the series we were traveling in Asia and received a State Department request that Gene and Jimmy travel to South Vietnam to visit with our troops. It just so happened that we were in Bangkok with Kathy Whitworth, Carol Mann and Sandra Haynie. Of course they were excited about going and our official contacts were happy to have them join us. The military orders were cut and the six of us were ready the next day, but just before we were scheduled to leave we got word that our trip was canceled because of what was referred to as "activity" taking place at the airport where we were scheduled to land.

Then there was Greece, where we faced a unique problem with Glyfada Golf Course. First of all, it had just been completed. In fact, the clubhouse was barely finished in time for our cocktail party scheduled for the evening before the match between Tony Lema and Roberto De Vicenzo. Due to an insufficient watering system, the course was completely burned out and everyone was concerned about how the fairways would look on television because tourism played a huge role in the Greek economy and officials had visions of golf dramatically increasing the tourism trade. Fortunately, I met up with a U.S. Air Force colonel who was about to play a round of golf and asked whether he knew of any crop-dusting planes that might be available. He knew one company, and we hired the plane and pilot and bought all the green paint we could find and sprayed the fairways. Believe me, the place did not come off looking like Augusta National, but no one ever knew or questioned what we did. De Vicenzo and Lema put on a great match, with Tony winning by a stroke, 66 to 67.

Because of our experience in Greece and other locations, we were always looking for a back-up golf course just in case some unexpected emergency reared its ugly head. One time George Rogers and I took a pre-production trip around the world, visiting the courses we were scheduled to play. We flew into Luxembourg one Sunday night and the next morning played 18 holes and finished in time to catch our plane to Brussels. Since we had a five-hour layover in Brussels, we played the Royal Belgique Golf Club and then returned to the airport in time to catch our flight to Hamburg. So, in one day, we flew into three countries and played a round of golf in two of them. That's a record I would not care to duplicate ... and one that helps explain why mine was a job millions of golfers would have loved.

Our match in Hamburg, Germany, was played between Jay Hebert and a young German professional, Freidel Schmaderer.

Jay was the defending champion of a tournament in Cleveland, so traveling to Hamburg was no easy task for him. He arrived late Monday evening for a Tuesday morning match. To say the least, he was exhausted. On top of that he would be playing a golf course he had never seen. Add to that the jet lag he was suffering after his long trip from the States, and he was in pretty poor shape.

For a while we thought Jay might not make it to the course in time for the match. If he hadn't, Sarazen would have substituted for him. Gene was ready for this because he had played with Schmaderer for three days and beat him badly each time. In fact, on a number of holes we could see Gene giving the young German some lessons. But Jay made it and Gene went back to announcing. However, the next day was a bad one for Jay and after nine holes he trailed his opponent. Naturally, the last thing that Jay wanted to do was to lose this nationally televised match to a player no one in the States had ever heard of before.

I decided as producer/director to do something about the situation. It was a beautiful day and after nine holes, it was approximately 3 p.m. and there was still plenty of time and sunlight to continue the match. But, at that point, to the amazement of everyone, I suspended play for the day. I announced that we were running low on film and that our delivery from the States had just arrived but had not yet cleared customs. As a result, we would stop filming and resume in the morning. It sounded pretty good to me, and no one objected. What really got me to act was something that happened on the ninth hole. Jay was so exhausted he could barely walk and on the green he lined up his putt and then addressed the ball. We waited for what seemed like minutes and finally Sarazen leaned over to me. "Fred, I think Jay is sleeping," he whispered. That did it. Jay finally came to life and putted out, but I had had enough and so had Jay. We got him back to the hotel and, after an early supper, he went straight to bed. The next morning he birdied the first three holes and won the match easily.

After the match, he was ready to party and he had no interest in getting the next plane back to the States. We were leaving for Copenhagen for a match with Tony Lema and Chris Paulson, a local pro, and Jay decided to join the crew and traveled with us to Denmark. I paid him $25, the fee we paid to local members of the gallery, and Jay came along with us.

You should have seen the expression on Lema's face when he saw Jay at the course.

"I thought I was playing a guy named Paulsen," Lema said. "What's Hebert doing here?"

I explained the situation and Tony calmed down. The next day, Tony, Gene and Jay played a practice round and we had a larger crowd following them around than we had for our match between Lema and Paulsen.

Our golfing caravan then visited Hong Kong for a match between Ted Kroll and Chen Ching Po. Since the Royal Hong

Kong Golf Club is situated near the border that separates Hong Kong from then Communist China, it had become a universal joke to remark that "if you slice one very wide off some of those tees — well, at least you will be one of the best golfers in Red China." In actuality, the border lies about three-and-half miles away. It is still close enough, however, for the golfer to see China in the distance beyond the mountains and, from the 17th green, see the small, white British gun emplacement near the top of those border peaks. In fact, the course's water supply comes from China via a giant pipeline.

While we were sitting around the club one day waiting for the now-familiar heavy rains to cease, we suddenly discovered that Sarazen was missing. Well, not really. But Gene, while sightseeing, had gotten the wrong transportation and ended up in mainland China. Obviously, he got back, but I am sure it is a mistake he wouldn't want to repeat.

It is taken for granted that when visiting Hong Kong, most male tourists make plans to have a suit of clothes made, since it only takes a couple of days. My 290-pound English cameraman, "Pinkie," decided that he would have a suit made. Unfortunately, Pinkie's fitting took place in his hotel room after a luncheon that was preceded by too many scotches and sodas. Pinkie retired to the couch in his room after lunch and spent the rest of the afternoon sleeping it off. In fact, he slept right through the appointment with his tailor. Imagine his surprise when a couple of days later, this beautiful pinstriped, blue suit arrived.

"Unfortunately," Pinkie explained, "it only looks good when I lie down on the couch, which is where I must have been when the tailor measured me. So, I shipped it off to my wife with instructions that I should be buried in it. At least, I'll always know that I went out as the best dressed man in the cemetery."

And, when Pinkie passed away, you know he actually did go out as the best dressed man in the place.

CHAPTER 2

Back in 1962 there were not many television sets around and not too many of us could afford the ones that were, so I often found myself watching the Shell shows at a bar in the Tudor City Hotel located on the East Side of New York City, where I happened to be living at the time.

On one particular Sunday afternoon I was at my favorite watering hole along with a couple of other golf addicts who had stopped by to watch the show and have a few beers.

That Sunday's match was between a future legend, Jack Nicklaus, and a present legend, Sam Snead. The match was being played at Pebble Beach and the two other customers were having a field day winning hole after hole in bets with the bartender.

When the match was over, the winners left and as the bartender poured me another beer he complained about how he had been wiped out by his friends. Since he mentioned that they were regulars, I suggested that perhaps in next week's match between Byron Nelson and a Dutchman named Gerry de Witt, he bet heavily on de Witt. In fact, I suggested that he bet that Nelson shoots an 80. He looked at me as if I was crazy and said that there is no way he would bet against his idol, Byron Nelson.

The following week I was at my usual seat at the bar and my bartender friend was betting heavily against Nelson. Byron made bogey after bogey and finally on the 18th hole, he hit a ball out of bounds and ended up shooting an 80.

After all the bets were paid off and his customers had left, the bartender came down to me and asked how I knew that Nelson was going to shoot 80? I told him that I was the producer-director of the series. He reached across the bar, grabbed my arm and pleaded with me: "Tell me what happens next week?" I just paid my check and left. I never did find out if he was going to bet on Phil Rodgers or Frank Phillips, an Asian champion, in a match from Singapore the following week.

As for Byron, well, you have no idea how many calls we got from him asking how much it would cost him to buy the negative of the show. He would have paid almost anything to keep it from airing on television.

The most popular of all the Shell shows was a classic match between Ben Hogan and Sam Snead, played at the Houston Country Club in 1964 and televised Feb. 21, 1965. The Houston Country Club had gold dust instead of sand in the traps and the greens are irrigated with oil. It is home base for those hackneyed caricatures, the Texas zillionaire and his lady, hung with ice cubes.

While the level of scoring was not overwhelming (Hogan shot 69 and Snead 72), the quality of golf was outstanding, especially from Hogan. In the years when he dominated the

American golf scene, Hogan was one of the great putters in the game, but as he grew older, his putting began to suffer from the "yips." The same can be said of many of the players on today's Champions Tour. Putting is often the first part of their game to go. But Hogan, at 52, remained a wonderful striker of the ball, and he still managed a golf course better than anyone who ever played, especially that day against Snead. I had been told that no man ever prepared himself better for a tournament than Hogan and as I watched him prepare for his match with Sam, I can believe it. He arrived in Houston four days before the filming began and prepared meticulously for the match. The result was a classic example of precision golf. Over 18 holes, Hogan never hit an approach shot more than 20 feet from the hole. He made three birdies without holing any sizable putts, and he hit all 18 greens and 14 fairways in regulation.

Shell always staged a luncheon in New York to introduce the series to the press each year. That year, the luncheon was held at the Waldorf Astoria and Sam Snead was our guest. As usual, we showed one of the films and it was the Snead vs. Hogan match. As the lights dimmed and the film came on, Sam was seen leaving the room. As he did, Red Smith, the famous sportswriter, asked Sam if he was planning to watch the film.

"No thank you, Red," Sam said. "I don't like losing to anyone and especially to Hogan and I don't like seeing it happen twice."

The press coverage of the Hogan-Snead match was unbelievable. In fact, Smith came down from New York to cover it. While it was our intention never to let the public know who had won any of the matches, we were more than happy to make an exception for the Houston match. We were flattered that a news-paperman of Red Smith's caliber would report it in *The New York Times* the following day. Following Red's death, the best of his stories were collected by his colleague and fellow Pulitzer Prize recipient, Dave Anderson, and published under the title, "The Red Smith Reader," and one of the selections was his reporting on the Snead match. The following is how his column appeared in *The New York Times* and in the collection:

> *"I am so glad I was able to see this match. I will remember it along with the War Admiral-Seabiscuit Match Race; Graziano-Zale; and Don Larsen's perfect game. Somebody told Fred Corcoran, who arranged the show for* Shell's Wonderful World of Golf, *that they ought to make it a series, best five out of nine. Somebody else suggested teaming Snead and Hogan against Arnold Palmer and Jack Nicklaus. If the round just filmed was the golfing equivalent of a Dempsey-Firpo rematch, the other would be like getting Dempsey and Joe Louis together. Only in golf is it possible to match the best of two eras. Hogan would be interested. He cannot resist a challenge."*

> *"Waiting at the 17th tee, a man said to Hogan: 'What a round you are having Ben! Sixteen holes and you have not missed a fairway, you have not missed a green, and you have not missed a putt.'"*

> *"I cannot afford to miss, or you get beat," Hogan said. The man answered, "And that is something that cannot be tolerated, eh?"*

> *"That's right," said Ben, unsmiling.*

Yes, having the great Red Smith in Houston was a special experience for all of us who had any association with the series.

For a couple of guys who were going to become a combined 104 years old in August (52 each, that is), Hogan and Snead looked remarkably youthful striding into the locker room after a two-day pitched battle on the fairways of the Houston Country Club.

Sam scowled blackly, disgusted with himself and furious at his long irons. Ben was imperturbable. Between them, they had played 67 years of professional golf and this was the first time the tight-lipped Hawk had whipped Snead in head-to-head combat. It was Hogan's first televised match and if any distractions could weaken his frightening self-discipline, they were all present here — frustrating delays, whining cameras, violently erratic weather. A cloudburst had halted play on the third hole, leaving the green drenched and the fairways deep in casual water. Then came scorching sunshine and the standard Texas wind.

Impervious to everything, Ben had played 18 perfect holes to beat par and Snead by three strokes with 69. "Beautiful round, Ben," said one old goat in the clubhouse, "but I was watching you putt back there on the 13th, and your stance was too open." The five-time U.S. Open champion kept a straight face realizing that although golf is a humbling game in Scotland, in Texas, "Humble" means an oil company.

Snead was disconsolate because his long irons got him into trouble four times, but he scrambled sensationally. The seventh hole, for example, is a dogleg to the left, around a thicket of tall trees. Hogan hit an iron to the corner of the dogleg and had an open shot to the green. Sam tried to clear the trees with a wood, hit a pine, and his ball bounced back toward the tee. It was not humanly possible to get home from there, but somehow he whistled his second shot through the trees to the edge of the green, beyond the last trap. "You dodged a bullet there," said Fred Corcoran, after Sam got down in two and halved the hole with a four.

For years I was asked what Hogan was really paid to play in that match against Snead. Let's face it, it was the only time that Ben had ever played in a match produced strictly for television. And it was also the last time.

In fact the match first telecast in 1965 had, for more than 30 years, never been repeated on television, thus denying millions of young golfers who never had the opportunity to see one of the greatest golfers of all time in action. Why? Because Hogan wouldn't allow it to be televised until late in his life. But the question remained: Was there extra incentive to encourage Ben to participate in the Shell series?

Since I signed and mailed out the checks to all the players, I knew that I had mailed one for $3,000 to Ben and one for $2,000 to Sam. If Ben had received any other compensation, it came from somewhere else. Sure enough, years after the series went off the air, I was having lunch with an old friend who was in a position to know if additional compensation had been passed on to Hogan. He admitted that AMF (which had purchased the Ben Hogan Company) was very interested in having Ben play that match — and to insure that he did, AMF paid him an additional $25,000.

Was this true? I'll never know, but as I think back and reflect on Ben's reluctance to display his game on network television, it made sense to me.

In the spring of 1963, Shell decided to conduct a nationwide survey of the public's reaction to *Shell's Wonderful World of Golf.* The study was conducted by the Opinion Research Corporation of Princeton, New Jersey. The following are just a few facts the study revealed:

- A total of 31 percent of the public had seen one or more shows by the time the 1963 season was over.
- Although the show had great appeal for golfers — 71 percent of the viewers were golfers — 26 percent of the viewers were from non-golfing households, and 16 percent of those had little or no interest in sports programs at all.
- About seven-tenths of the total audience were people in non-golf households.
- Research conducted some six months after the 1963 shows went off the air indicated that 24 percent of the public recalled viewing *Shell's Wonderful World of Golf.*
- People who had seen *Shell's Wonderful World of Golf* registered considerable interest in the travelogues dealing with the countries where the matches were played. A total of 74 percent found those segments to be "very interesting." The "very interesting" was quite high — 61 percent — among people who knew that Shell was the sponsor.

• In the fall of 1963, correct sponsor identification was made by 13 percent of those who recalled viewing the show. In that same year, correct sponsor identification of two other golf shows — *All Star Golf* and *Challenge Golf* — was one percent or less. In fact, Shell was often named as the sponsor of All Star Golf and the Challenge Golf series. In terms of numbers of audience, about 5.7-million people correctly identified the sponsor. Naturally, this delighted everyone involved in Mr. Spaght's pet project ... especially me.

George Rogers left the series after five years and was succeeded by Jimmy Demaret, who instantly added a new and welcome dimension to the show. His wit and humor, his smile and willingness to cooperate were most welcomed since George's and Gene's relationship could be difficult. As you would expect, Gene was a very competitive person and he often felt that George — who wasn't remotely in Gene's class as a golfer — tried to undermine him in the editing process. He often complained that George was responsible for many of Gene's best lines being left on the cutting room floor. This wasn't true, but I'll be candid and admit that my life became a hell of a lot easier when George left and Jimmy Demaret came on board.

At times I thought I was producing the "Odd Couple" version of golf with Jimmy and Gene. They were about as different as two people could possibly be, but they got along famously. The shows took on a lighter touch. In addition to great golf and great courses and great travelogues, we now added fun and laughter — which is just what we hoped for with Jimmy at the microphone.

Jimmy could and did go on and on with one funny line after another.

For example:

On ... the golf club: "It should be held softly, like a lady."

On ... golfer's clothes: "In the early days, golfers all dressed like pall bearers."

On ... Sam Snead's croquet-style putting: "Sam looks like he is basting a turkey."

On ... traveling the Tour: "In the early days we couldn't afford a major credit card, so I carried an Oklahoma Credit Card — a gasoline siphon hose."

On ... Jackie Burke Jr.: "Jackie's father asked me to babysit Jackie. I didn't realize I'd end up babysitting for him for the next 50 years."

On ... the Onion Creek Course: "God put it here, all I did was manicure it."

On ... Phil Harris: "Phil can drink more than Dean Martin with one lip tied behind his back."

On ... Harris' favorite drink: "The next one."

On ... Bob Hope's golf game: "Bob has a wonderful short game. Too bad it's off the tee."

On ... locker rooms years ago: "In the old days, the locker rooms not only looked dreary, but they stunk."

On ... any golf course: "A golf course is a great equalizer. It brings you down to earth, whether your name is Eisenhower, Palmer or Schultz."

On ... the integrity of the game: "Golf is based on honesty. In what other sport would anyone admit to a seven on an easy par-3 hole."

On ... his philosophy: "I lived by a paraphrase of the old biblical law: 'An eye for an eye, a tooth for a tooth.' I went by a joke for a joke."

On ... golf shot description: "Fringe around the green is frog hair," "Topped shots are 'worm burners.'" "Testy short putts are 'white knucklers.'"

On ... not winning more tournaments: "I'm not sure I would have won more tournaments had I taken the game more seriously. Maybe I wouldn't have won as many. I had fun at night and I do know that I had to withdraw from the last round in some tournaments I was winning because I was suffering from terrible hangovers."

On ... Bob Hope and Bing Crosby: "I get them mixed up. One of them thinks he is funny but can't sing. The other isn't funny but thinks he can sing."

On ... his wardrobe: "In 1954, I owned 43 hats, 71 pairs of slacks, 20 jerseys, 55 shirts and 39 sports jackets. I was partial to brick red, mulberry, royal crimson, pale pink, purple, hunter green and flaming scarlet. I learned about colors from my father, who was a painter. In fact, he was the Rembrandt of House Painters.

Filming a match presents its own set of problems. With seven cameras in action, each operator becomes a director on his own. Every shot was photographed. We skipped nothing. We exposed approximately 30,000 feet of 16 millimeter color film per show.

Since we mounted our cameras on vehicles and tracks, we had to camouflage them and this became quite an operation. Our technical group included two Hollywood camouflage men who had been doing this type of work for many years. They had to match their camouflage material with the golf course. Erecting the portable platforms took us only minutes. Then the "greens men," with the assistance of local hired help, started chopping down branches and other essential foliage. It was kept moist until the day before the match, then it was mounted to the vehicles and tracks so that the viewers got the impression they were actually seeing a native bush or tree instead of our cameras. Occasionally, this created problems since once a shot was filmed, they moved down the fairway, usually to the green for their next position. Once in South America, Roberto De Vicenzo's drive hit a truck and buried in our camouflage. Not realizing this, the camera operator ordered his driver to drive down to the green. De Vicenzo's caddie took off after the truck, only to be stopped by Roberto.

"Let him go," Roberto said. "It's the first time I ever hit a 450-yard drive from tee to green."

On another occasion, in Ireland, two women who were facing an urgent call from nature, spotted what they thought was a convenient tree. You can imagine their embarrassment when the tree suddenly drove away.

We often hired local bilingual interpreters to help us organize our galleries. You should have seen them with a walkie-talkie in one hand and a bullhorn in the other, acting like Cecil B. De Mille. Sometimes it was more of a problem corralling them than it was the gallery. Our nicest experience was in Hamburg, Germany, where we were supplied with very pretty female college students as interpreters. You should have seen our crew pay attention to them — not a goof all the way.

Sometimes the players spent considerable time in the woods. We would move our cameras and microphones hoping to catch the action. Hackers shouldn't feel badly: one of the pros actually lost his ball in the Alps at the Villa D'Este Golf Course in Italy. Fifty of us looked and looked, but to no avail. On film, it's rather amusing to see so many people going in and coming out of the woods looking for a golf ball without any luck.

There have been other situations, too. For example, we were flying from Los Angeles to New York to South America. For some strange reason, our equipment — and it was no small package — never got off the plane in New York and was flown back to Los Angeles. You can imagine the reaction of our unit manager on location when the crew arrived in Argentina without a bit of equipment. It was almost like, "No tickee, no shirtee."

There were times when it took as much as eight to 10 hours to clear customs with our equipment. We also had talent problems with customs, too. For example, one year Dave Marr arrived in London and was greeted by a very cheery customs inspector. Noticing the golf bag with his name on the side, he politely started asking questions.

"I assume you will be playing one of our fabulous courses while you are visiting London?" he asked.

"Yes, I will," said Dave.

"How much will you get paid?" inquired the inspector.

"That depends on whether I win or lose," said Dave.

"And do you have a work permit to enter this country?" asked the inspector.

Dave was flabbergasted and within a matter of minutes, the eager inspector had him booked on the next plane back to the United States. Fortunately, the next plane did not leave until the next day. The customs officer confiscated his passport, but agreed to let Dave and his wife move to the airport hotel for the night rather than rest in the local jail. Bright and early the next morning, Shell made arrangements for us to rescue public enemy Marr and all was well. However, as far as Dave was concerned, the straw that broke the camel's back took place when he returned to the customs office for his passport.

"I am sorry for the inconvenience," the inspector said. "Perhaps if you had been Ben Hogan or Arnold Palmer, I would have recognized you and there would have been no problem at all."

Then there was our problem in Trinidad. The course had burned out completely and was unplayable. We learned this when we were in Maracaibo, Venezuela, the day before we were scheduled to leave for the island. We kept the crew and equipment in Venezuela while our Shell representative and I went out to the airport to catch a 10 o'clock flight to check out the situation. The plane was late leaving Panama City and did not arrive in Maracaibo until midnight. We arrived in Trinidad at 5 a.m. and by 11 a.m. our worst fears were confirmed. The course was unplayable. Now, we had to find another golf course and figure out what to do with my crew, which was happily lounging around the pool at the Hotel Del Largo in Maracaibo.

We were notified by Shell's New York office to fly to Nassau. Have you ever tried to go to Nassau from Trinidad after midnight on Saturday? Forget it! We traveled with the same BOAC (now British Air) crew from Trinidad to Antigua to Barbados to Bermuda and finally off to Nassau the next day. So much for the glamorous world of television. Another transportation nightmare took place during our match in Monaco. All the Italian airlines were on strike and since we had commitments in Villa D'Este, we had to find other means of transportation. The trains were full, so we hired a huge bus, loaded the two rear rows of seats with hero sandwiches and beer and started off on a 10-hour trip to northern Italy. Surprisingly enough, we had a ball — but please, I would never want to do it again.

Being associated with *Shell's Wonderful World of Golf* was an experience as well as an education. I will never forget and will always appreciate my meeting with Mr. Spaght at Giambelli's Restaurant in New York City. We talked about the series and then he asked, "Fred, forgetting the monetary gain you have made from the series, what was the most gratifying and memorable thing you can remember about *Shell's Wonderful World of Golf*?" I told him: "As a result of my experiences and the people I had met on my travels around the world with the show, I knew that I could travel just about any place in the world, feeling confident that when I arrived in that strange country I could count on some familiar face waiting for me and whisking me through customs."

Of course, travel wasn't our only headache. We also had many editing problems back in New York. One in particular stands out.

It was the first year of the series and as we prepared for our first show to be televised, Herb Wind and I held a private screening for Mr. Spaght and a few other Shell and K & E executives. I could tell from Mr. Spaght's reactions that he was quite pleased so you can imagine my surprise when the screening ended and he looked right at me.

"Fred, you and your team have done a magnificent job," he said. "I'm sure the golfing public as well as the network will be excited about the program. However, there is one problem and you really must eliminate it before the show goes on the air or I will not allow it to go on the air. The problem is — and I apologize for not bringing it up at the time — but someplace in the show there is a split infinitive and it must come out. I cannot have school teachers in Wichita or anyplace else in the United States writing me letters about it."

I quickly assured Mr. Spaght that it would come out.

The truth is, I didn't know what a split infinitive was. When I returned to the office, I called Herb, who was absolutely seething. There was no way, he said, that he would write a split infinitive into the script. Eventually, I recovered. After all, this was only Monday, and we'd certainly find it by Thursday, which was my deadline for delivering our show to CBS. The next day, we set aside the travelogue and the commercials and started to screen the show. Herb screened it at least twice and emphatically announced that there were no split infinitives in the show. Now I really had a problem. Who was to tell the President of Shell Oil — and an honor student at Stanford at that — that he was wrong? First I called my contacts at K & E and Shell and told them that we were unable to find the offending split infinitive. Their reply was simply that if Mr. Spaght heard it, it must be there, so find it. Completely frustrated at this point and not knowing what to do, I called the English Department at Columbia University, explained my predicament, and offered to pay a professor $75 (which was a lot of money in those days) if someone would come down and review the show. I also suggested they bring some official stationary as I was going to need written support if they could not resolve the problem. Well, the professor arrived, sat down in the screening room, viewed the show twice and offered to dictate a letter stating that he could not find a single split infinitive in the show. I rushed off a copy to K & E and to Shell but to no avail. Either we find Mr. Spaght's split infinitive or there would be no show. Period.

Now it was Wednesday and CBS was frantically waiting for the film. They had six delay markets that were waiting for their 16mm prints and time was running out. I was finally desperate enough to do something that could cost me my job, but I felt that I had no choice. I called Mr. Spaght's office and asked his secretary what his schedule was for the next few days. She informed me that he was leaving for London and would be gone for a week. That's all I had to know. I told my editing crew to put the travelogue and the commercials back in the show and let's get the hell out of here. Mr. Spaght wouldn't see it and those other clowns wouldn't know a split infinitive from the works of Shakespeare. After all, if they knew where it was, wouldn't they have been a hero and solved the mystery days ago?

At this point, let me pause and go back about a month, when

I was having a drink with one of my editors. He told me that his son, who had recently graduated from college as an honor student majoring in English, was a very low-handicap golfer who wanted, of all things, to work in the film business. I suggested that he bring his son in, give him a broom and let him learn the business working around the editing room. If you have ever spent any time in an editor's cutting room, you'd know why I suggested the broom. I started in the editing room and that's where I learned what the business was all about, so naturally, I thought it was a good place for him to start as well. By the time of my split infinitive dilemma, this young man had been assigned to checking on the quality of the prints before they left the shop, so as you can see he advanced rapidly.

Anyway, the elements of the show were all back together again — the travelogue, the commercials and the show itself and my hero is checking the show for any lighting or sound problems we might have. "If you should find a split infinitive, please let me know," I said as I closed the door and headed down the hall. About 30 minutes later, he walked into my office.

"Hey, Fred," he said "I don't know whether you are serious about that split infinitive, but if you are, I found it."

I almost fell out of my chair.

"WHERE"? I screamed.

He said it was in the commercial that the agency sent over. I should have known. We had stripped the film of both commercials and the travelogue and just concentrated on the show, which is why everyone missed it. I rushed to the phone and as calmly as I could told that so and so at the agency that we found the problem and that it was in the commercial. I also told him that the show was at CBS and when they had corrected the error, they should rush the revised commercial to the network.

What was the split infinitive? I believe it was "to more better inform."

I believe that the reaction of the viewers and media was best summed up by writer Bob Sommers, who in the winter of 1982 wrote in *The Met Golfer* magazine: "Rather than risk terminal frostbite with a Sunday afternoon stroll one frosty February day in 1965, I turned on the television set and watched Chi Chi Rodriguez and Tommy Jacobs play a Shell match at the Lyford Cay Club in Nassau. It was cold. Through my window I could see shaggy blades of brownish grass poking through a thin layer of snow, but there they were, playing golf in short sleeves in the Bahamas on *Shell's Wonderful World of Golf.*"

It's funny how some things linger in your memory. While the series was on the air for nine years and ran through 92 matches (and I saw everyone of them), the memory of that match in Nassau has stayed with me. Why? Certainly not because of the golf, because Jacobs shot a 70 and Rodriguez a 74 and I cannot remember a single shot they played. It did not rank near the quality of the match that Ben Hogan played against Sam Snead. I think it might have been the policeman in his natty white helmet, directing the traffic on Bay Street; or the crowd milling around the straw market; or the statue of Columbus in front of the government building high on the hill overlooking the harbor; or the statue of Queen Victoria watching the horse-drawn carriages bearing tourists out to Fort Finley. All of those things were included in that one hour on Sunday afternoon because Shell gave us a taste of the country where the matches were being played, along with a look at one of the world's great golf courses.

Over lunch not long ago, somebody described it as a "neat show." It was neat, yes, but it was more than that. It was the best-filmed golf show ever produced. The sorrow of it all is that it could never be done again. Producing another series like that would cost more than World War II. Actually, because of the improved efficiency and the lessons we learned from our mistakes, the budget never really varied. It was under $1 million in the first year and it was around $1.3 million in the last year, even though prize money increased significantly. In the beginning, winners received $3,000 and losers $2,000. At the end the winner got $7,000 and the loser got $3,000. In the last two years, we evolved into an elimination tournament, where the eventual winner took home $37,000.

Everyone in our profession was envious of us and our assignment. We got to see the world; we got to play many of the world's most famous golf courses and we met lovely women all over the world (although they wouldn't get a second look on Fifth Avenue). We were accused of being gourmets (although we often suffered from "Deli Belly") and of course we stayed in the most magnificent and glamorous hotels around the world. Like the time we stayed in a country for eight days and were without water of any kind for six of the eight days. Prior to leaving, one of our crewmembers purchased nine bottles of Vichy water and proceeded to take a bath.

Every show proved to be a series of headaches — but never a bore!

There were often multi-lingual misunderstandings and confusion.

In South America, the customs problem was insurmountable. In order to make a fairly quick getaway we bought several new suitcases, loaded the bottoms with film cans, the top with clothing and hoped that the customs inspectors would just give us cursory looks. Outside, we had a couple of station wagons warming up. We got through ... luckily.

Whenever a player faced a trouble shot, we always had Gene interview him to see how the player planned to play the shot.

One such interview took place at the Glyfada Golf Club in a match that featured Tony Lema playing Roberto De Vicenzo. Roberto had hit a tee shot just inches away from a wire fence. Gene cornered De Vicenzo at the spot where his ball lay.

"Well Roberto," he said, "You don't have such a bad lie. How are you going to play the shot?"

Roberto looked at the ball and the fence, then took the microphone from Gene and handed him his club.

"Here, Gene," Roberto said, "you hit and I talk."

In 1967, our series included a visit to Rome and an exciting match between Bruce Devlin and Tommy Jacobs at the Golf Club of Rome.

The match went down to the final putt, with Jacobs making a birdie for the win. What made all of this worth noting was the fact that my assistant director, Dick Ashe, was standing next to me near the green when Tommy won the match. When the show was telecast the following January, I received a call at home from Dick just as the show went off the air.

"Fred!" screamed Ashe. "What did you do to the show?"

I was confused and asked him what he was talking about. He explained that he was standing next to me at 18 and he swore that it was Bruce who sank the winning putt.

"No," I told Dick, "it was Tommy."

I asked why he was so upset. Apparently, his brother was a very heavy gambler and had bet heavily on Devlin based on the erroneous information Dick had given him. The last I heard from Dick Ashe he was heading out of town before his brother caught up with him.

One of my saddest memories was of a match between Peter Alliss and Tony Lema at Bermuda's Mid-Ocean Club. Our filming of the match took place just a couple of weeks before Lema and his wife died in a plane crash.

Prior to the match, Tony was his usual jovial self and my last memory of him will always be my best. I bought him a bottle of champagne at dinner the night before the match. He matched my generosity. Then someone else did. Boy, were we hung over the next day — including both Tony and Peter.

The match got off to a fast start with both Tony and Peter making birdies on the second hole, but after making a birdie on the sixth, Tony was one stroke up. On the par-3 seventh, he ran into big trouble when his tee shot flew over the green and finished on the downslope of a bunker behind the green. It was a very difficult shot, and he couldn't quite pull it off. He left it in the trap. His next shot from the sand was a beauty, but it was too late. He made a bogey and the match was level.

On the back nine, Alliss had many opportunities to move ahead of Tony, but his putting failed him on at least four consecutive holes (it might have been the champagne) and he missed his chance for birdies. Tony had been on the ropes for most of the back nine, but Peter could not administer the knockout blow. At No. 17, Lema rebounded and made a 15-footer for birdie and took a one-stroke lead with one hole to play. Alliss made his par on the beautiful finishing hole and Tony had only to make a three-footer to win the match. But it was not to be and, fittingly, the match ended in a tie.

Mickey Wright, arguably the finest woman golfer in history, was invited to play twice on *Shell's Wonderful World of Golf.*

In her first match, she defeated France's Brigette Varangot in their match at the Club de Golf — Estoril in Portugal, which Mickey won. Perhaps it was because this was the first women's match in the Shell series or because of Mickey's reputation, but for years this show was one of the most requested shows in our Shell library.

Mickey returned a couple of years later to defeat the fine Canadian champion, Marlene Streit, at the Toronto Golf Club in Canada. At the completion of the first nine holes, it was obvious that Mickey was playing outstanding golf, while Marlene was not having one of her better days.

Before the players teed off on the back nine, I suggested that this might be a good opportunity to turn the final nine holes of play into a golf clinic. We filmed more slow motion shots on the back nine than we ever had before, and with Mickey's fine play, we had a very good clinic from Mickey on how to play golf. Marlene, on the other hand, gave a good example of how wrong a match could go when you are having a bad day.

We even had problems with our spelling. One year Shell arranged for us to have our own plane. It wasn't a jet, since they were still new and certainly would not fit into our budget, even given Shell's generosity, but having our plane gave us the luxury of not being locked into airline schedules, economy-class seating on long flights and allowed us to arrange our own meals. It also meant that occasionally members of the crew could bring their wives and organize parties and so on, which did wonders for domestic tranquility.

The minute the contract was signed with Global Airways we sent a crew over to paint "Shell's Wonderful World of Golf" on the plane. We then flew from New York to Argentina to Brazil and back to Miami, where someone from the control tower called to our pilot as we were coming to our gate.

"Can't you guys from Shell spell?" the man said.

It seems that our sign painter had spelled "Wonderful" with two L's, so we had traveled thousands of miles advertising the fact that we were "Shell's *Wonderfull* World of Golf!"

It's a good thing Mr. Spaght didn't see that!

Sarazen gave a priceless examination of some of the world's greatest — and occasionally unknown — courses. Happily they coincided with some of our most memorable matches.

As I wrote earlier, one of our matches was played on the famed Mid-Ocean Club on the island of Bermuda, a glittering jewel set in solitary splendor in the Atlantic Ocean. Gene was especially fond of Mid-Ocean.

"I traveled the world over and yet there is nothing to compare with beautiful Bermuda," said Sarazen. "It's been a few years since my last visit to Mid-Ocean but there is still the surprising hilly terrain, which means a number of blind shots from the tee and steeply banked fairways that call for careful placements of shots to take advantage of the roll. There are many bunkers, big and small, 18 on the first hole alone, and in some cases only a narrow strip of sand lies between you and the ever-present, blue-green Atlantic.

"While there is an ocean, there is also inland water like the lake on the fifth hole," Sarazen continued. "I consider this to be one of the toughest holes in golf. The breezes off the Atlantic are a constant companion. They get pretty strong at times, so you must keep the ball low under the wind. The greens were built into the contours of the land. Don't be surprised if you see a single putt go uphill, downhill and break sideways as well."

Gene was right. Bermuda has a special flavor and a feeling about it. And the Mid-Ocean Club plays a prominent part in the island's romantic tradition.

Another memorable Sarazen course description was of the Golf Club de Pen. A demandingly narrow course cut through the heather and glacial mounds, the site of a match between Peter Thomson, who won the British Open a phenomenal five times, and popular American professional Dave Marr, winner of the 1965 PGA Championship.

"The Holland we hear about has as many canals as roads and so flat that you can see from one end to the other. And you expect to find golf courses to match, but the old world still has some surprises in it. The Golf Club de Pen is one of them. The land here was at the southern tip of the last great glacier. When the ice moved down from the north it pushed the sandy soil ahead of it into the rolling hilly terrain. What were once sand dunes are now high grass mounds that guard the corners of the doglegs, produce a number of blind approaches to the greens, provide elevated views of the course and form holes so narrow that driving a golf ball is like threading a candle through the eye of a needle.

"You know, some golf historians claim that the game was first played right here in Holland. Maybe yes and maybe no, but in any case this course is proof that the Dutch of today appreciate a real golfing challenge."

Marr took a one-stoke lead early in that match, but on the fifth hole Dave got into trouble. He drove far to the right and tried to carry a 9-iron over a tall tree directly in his line to the green but came up short and lost the hole. Thomson bogeyed the sixth hole to go one down and then on the seventh hole Marr moved two strokes ahead with a birdie. Thomson was two down at the turn but both players' ability to play trouble shots was displayed at the par-5 11th hole. After hooking his drive amidst a lot of loose twigs, Marr slashed a 4-iron back into the fairway and went on to get his par. On the 13th hole, Dave got it together again, making his second long putt of the day for a birdie. He now led by three strokes and it appeared to be all over for Thomson when on the 16th he drove poorly into the deep heather. But Thomson recovered with a great 9-iron, a phenomenal shot that turned imminent disaster into a new life. Thomson made his putt for birdie and on the very next hole made another birdie. But Marr rose to the challenge with his own birdie. Marr went on to win the match by four strokes, but it was one of our most dramatic shows.

Another of Gene's memorable course descriptions came in a match between "himself"— Ireland's Christy O'Connor Sr. — and PGA champion Don January at Royal County Down in Northern Ireland.

"You ever wonder what playing golf on the moon might be like?" Gene said. "You get an idea when you play some of the holes on the Royal County Down course. But without turning your head, you know exactly where you are. You are in Northern Ireland where the hills are a color of green you find nowhere else. Built in 1899 by Old Tom Morris from St. Andrews, this is not only a very scenic place to play golf, it is and always has been a vigorous championship test and has been the site of many important tournaments. Take the ninth hole for example, for the first 100 yards or so it seems like just another golf hole. Then you come upon a spectacular view. Long fairways with the Morne Mountains as a backdrop — the Irish Sea to one side — a 426-yard par-4 that requires strong play from tee to green. The dunes have provided many natural elevations from which to drive but have also created some fine approaches. A little local knowledge would not hurt here. Built on dunes land, you expect plenty of bunkers — and you get them. The 18th hole has almost 20 bunkers staggered all the way down the line, so this course of more than 6,700 yards, a par-71, takes the best golf you can muster — a little Irish luck, too!"

Gene certainly saw some of the Irish luck rub off on January. His second shot to the first green caught a bunker 20 yards from the pin and Don was faced with one of the toughest shots in all of golf. He exploded out well but left himself at least 30 feet short of the hole. After O'Connor made his par five, January had a long putt for a birdie. His ball hit the back of the cup, jumped up like a kangaroo and fell back down into the hole. January had a two-stroke lead going into the par-3 fourth hole and was faced with a 30-foot downhill approach putt on a fast green, which he sank it to go two under par and three shots ahead of O'Connor.

On the par-4 fifth hole Christy missed another green in regulation and Don was on in two and Christy was on a mound about 100 feet from the cup. He took a 9-iron for his third shot. He chipped it up and ran it well past the hole and he had to settle for still another bogey. While all that was going on, Don had a 20-footer for another birdie. He now had his magic putter going for him as he sank his putt for his third birdie in the match and a commanding five-stroke lead after only five holes of play.

Christy tried to make it interesting. He had a real good drive on the par-4 11th hole of almost 285 yards, leaving a short approach to the green. His 9-iron was heading right for the hole, but the ball lipped the right hand corner of the cup. Christy made his birdie and trailed January by just four. On the 12th hole, both players were putting for birdies, Christy missed that attempt and Don picked up still another shot as he converted his birdie to again lead by five shots. And on the next hole O'Connor used a 7-iron on his approach to the green and the fine Irish professional again took aim at the pin. It landed just short of the green, ran up on line 20 feet from the cup. After January hit the green in two and putted for his par, Christy stepped up for his birdie try. His countrymen watched hopefully as he bent over the ball — he made a fine stroke and the ball disappeared into the cup for birdie to cut the margin again to four. There were no further changes in the match over the next few holes and January continued to play superb golf, shooting a 68 to defeat O'Connor.

The Olympic Club in San Francisco, the scene of multiple U.S. Opens, is still a demanding test of golf. This match was between the winner of more international championships than any other player, Roberto De Vicenzo from Buenos Aires, Argentina, and his opponent, one of the finest shotmakers on the tour, Ryder Cupper and lawyer, Dan Sikes of Jacksonville, Florida.

On the second hole Roberto had a 15-footer for a birdie — he canned it to go one stroke up in the match. However, on the fourth Sikes banged his approach to the long par-4 green within easy birdie range for his three to tie De Vicenzo. After Roberto bogeyed the sixth, Sikes gave one back on No. 9. His second shot to the green ran all the way through the gallery and down the embankment, leaving Sikes about 35 feet from the cup. He made an excellent chip from there and missed a very short putt and after nine holes he led by a single stroke. Hosts Demaret and Sarazen talked with Sikes about that missed putt.

"Dan, you know what Roberto was saying that if you and he were just playing around, he would have given you that putt and I was saying it's almost what we would have termed as a 'gimme.'" Replied Sikes, "Well that's true, Gene, but there are no gimmes. The grain of the grass took the ball. I was expecting it to run straight in and I should have hit it a little firmer."

On the 12th hole after Sikes bogeyed, Roberto's fine chip almost went in the hole. He got his par and the match was even. This see-saw match finally tilted towards Sikes on the par-5 16th. He had a half wedge and pulled it way left and was faced with a long putt for a birdie. After De Vicenzo got his par, Dan hit his 25-footer into the hole for a birdie four and took a one-stroke lead in the match. On the 17th hole, Dan's beautiful wedge left him within eight feet of the cup and his second consecutive birdie to lead by two strokes going into the last hole.

And then on to 18, Dan got lucky again. He hit his drive into the dark of the forest, but the trees sent it right back into the sunlight. Roberto's drive was in the center of the fairway. With not much room to come home, Dan took out an iron — it looked liked he was headed to a bunker, but Lady Luck paid him a visit once more. His ball just missed the trap. Roberto was in excellent position to get back in the match. He used a wedge but again pulled his ball way left, landing just short of Dan's ball. He settled for a par 72 for the match. With victory within his grasp here at 18, Sikes had no intention of getting the ball up in the air, so he selected his putter and made his par to defeat De Vicenzo. At the completion of the match, Demaret asked Sikes what was the difference between playing golf and being a lawyer and Dan replied, "About 75K a year."

One visit took us to Germany and the city of Frankfurt on the river Marne, and the Frankfurter Golf Club, a par-72 layout with tons of trees and a whole lot of bunkers. The match was between Harold Henning, the winner of the German Open and six-time Canada Cup competitor from South Africa, and Doug Sanders of the United States.

Sarazen describes this interesting course as follows:

"Golf is prospering almost everywhere in the world, and Germany is no exception. Of the many beautiful courses in this country, certainly one of the finest is the Frankfurter Golf Club. Over 50 years old, its established championship character and rugged elegance is more than enough to satisfy anyone that desires golf at its best. Trees are one of the course's major characteristics. These tall, thin evergreens are spotted everywhere on the course and there is a whole forest of other trees that line nearly every fairway. Some holes are enclosed entirely by woods, like the beautiful 10th. Bunkering is a second important feature, particularly around the greens, which are extremely well bunkered. These deep traps have very high walls. Getting out of them takes all the skill you can muster. The course plays just under 6,500 yards long and par is 72."

Stepping to the tee as the epitome of sartorial perfection was Doug Sanders. Nattily attired, he looked like a Texas pink grapefruit. As Gene said to Demaret, "Between you and Sanders, I thought I would have to wear colored glasses here today in Frankfurt."

Both Sanders and Henning drove well on the first hole and they both made pars, but on the second hole, Harold drove into serious trouble on the left. He didn't have a clear shot and his ball

64

was in deep grass, but he decided to try a 4-wood anyway and not surprisingly it did not work out too well. He pulled the ball way left and for his third shot he had tall trees directly in his line to the green. So Henning decided to play in the opposite direction to get more room to work with. He ended up making a triple-bogey seven on the hole while Doug made four. Both Sanders and Henning birdied the fifth hole and made pars on Nos. 6, 7 and 8. And then at the par-4 ninth Sanders had this 8-iron approach to the green. It was a beauty that led to a birdie and a two-under-par 34 on the front nine. Sanders had it all going and on the 11th hole Doug had a putt for a birdie but he missed it.

Sanders hooked his drive on the 14th but he got a lucky break as his ball bounced off a tree and back into the open. From there Doug hit an excellent 8-iron approach, taking full advantage of his luck by holing the putt for a birdie from 20 feet away. By then the match was really over, Sanders had a five-stroke lead with four holes to play. It was Henning's poor driving and Sanders' fine play that won the match for him as he shot a splendid 68.

The Peachtree Golf Club was the site for the 18-hole match between one of golf's all-time great champions, the legendary Sam Snead, and two-time U.S. Open champion Julius Boros.

On the par-5 second hole, Sam hit his wedge shot of about 70 yards to pin high, about eight feet from the flagstick. He birdied the hole for a one-stroke lead in the match. After Boros bogeyed the fourth hole Sam took a commanding lead early in the match. He drove about 270 yards off the tee and had just enough clearance for his second shot. He used a 2-wood from the right rough and landed just short of the green and from there got down in two for another birdie and a three-stroke lead over Boros. Demaret analyzed Snead's and Boros' use of the toughest club in the bag.

"The 1-iron is a tough club to use. Its extremely straight face and its narrow blade requires a lot of hand action at impact. Sam's swing worked well until he reached the hitting area. Here he failed to get his right hand through in time and the ball started out well right of the green. Julius, who uses a lot of hand action, got them working very well. At impact his hands banged good and solid through the shot and he got the ball started to the green." Sam's 1-iron finished well right of the green and he took a bogey. Boros hit the green and two-putted for a par. Snead was now two shots up.

On the 10th hole Sam needed a putt for his third consecutive birdie on a par-5 hole and he got it to once again lead by three. On the par-3 11th hole, Sam pushed his shot far off to the right and settled in the rough about 30 yards from the pin. His second shot stopped about 15 feet from the hole. From there Snead three-putted for a double bogey and Boros, who parred the hole, was right back in the hunt, just one stroke back. Both players got their pars on the 12th hole and there was no change in the match. But on the 14th, Boros got his par while Sam three-putted again for a bogey and the match was even. Then on the par-5 16th hole, Snead hit two tremendous shots into the wind and reached the green in two. He made his fourth birdie of the day on the par-5 holes for a one-stroke lead with just two to play and Snead went on to win by two.

Bobby Jones, a member of Peachtree, where the Snead-Boros

match took place, made his first impression on the American sports public as a 14-year-old at the 1916 U.S. Amateur at Merion, where he won two matches before losing to the defending champion in the quarterfinals. His beautiful, rhythmic swing and natural instincts for the game began to pay off seven years later. It was the 1923 U.S. Open and in the field were his formidable contemporaries, Walter Hagen and Sarazen. But Bob beat everyone to capture his first national championship. Over the next seven seasons he won the U.S. Amateur five times, the U.S. Open three more times, three British Opens and a British Amateur. Along with his remarkable record, he set new standards of sportsmanship as well.

Wherever he played, at home or abroad, Jones was followed by huge, devoted galleries. In the spring of 1930, he sailed for Great Britain and won both the British Amateur at St. Andrews and the British Open at Hoylake. On his return, Bobby received a ticker-tape parade in New York City, and then it was back to business again. He won the U.S. Open at Interlachen Country Club with the help of a magnificent birdie putt on the last green. Then, finally, Jones returned to Merion where it all began and won the U.S. Amateur to complete the Grand Slam. It was a dramatic climax to his career, and immediately afterwards, he retired from active competition.

Let's go back to 1966 when he relived memories with Sarazen at the Peachtree Golf Club in Atlanta.

Gene: "You know we had some things in common. We played in our first Open in 1920, were born a couple of weeks apart, and married two great girls."

Bob: "It looks like we handled things pretty well."

Gene: "Yeah, we did a pretty good job."

Bob: "I don't know what the girls think about it!"

Gene: "Another thing, Bob, I recall the early days when you and I played in the Open at Columbia, we were both a couple of club throwers and we said, now look, if you throw a club, you pay me $5 and if I throw a club, I pay you $5. I don't think I've thrown a club since."

Bob: "Well, I have, but we didn't that day."

Gene: "Will you ever forget the time you walked into the railroad station with O.B. Keeler and you saw me in my knickers with the Open Championship cup? You looked at it and said I would like to play you for that tomorrow."

Bob: "Well, I had already played you for it that day when you won it because I really didn't have the right to say that."

Gene: "Bob, golf has come a long way since then. Television has been a great contributor and I think one of the outstanding personalities is your friend President Eisenhower, who did a great job to push golf along while he was President."

Bob: "Yes, that's right, he certainly did. But you know television I think has been responsible for the improved understanding of the swing. I think now you see so many good players and you see good swings around public courses and country clubs that you did not see before and I think television has had a lot to do with that."

I believe that was Jones' last appearance on television. He passed away in 1971.

In Wales, with its splendid landscape radiating a lyrical elegance and in harmony with the land, the Southern Down Golf Club was the setting for the match between Canada Cup competitor and winner of the French, Belgian and Italian Opens Welshman Dave Thomas, and PGA Champion and Ryder Cupper Bob Rosburg.

Sarazen described the beautiful Welsh layout.

"Welsh shepherds have been allowed free grazing on this land since the days of William the Conqueror. The sheep have as much right to the golf course as the members, but no one really minds. They save a lot of mowing costs and are an important part of this course's excellent condition. The sheep grazing here emphasize the point that this is a natural golf course. It represents a time when golf was played in its purest surroundings. No bulldozer ever flattened out this naturally rolling terrain. Where there was a mound like this one that splits the 18th fairway in two, it was left intact. The result is a unique golf hole which can be played several different ways and if you get off line you are sure to get tangled up in the most typical of bushes in the British Isles — gorse. And to top it off, you almost never play a round on a quiet, windless day. It is no accident that these pins have rubber near the base to prevent them from breaking off when the high winds blow. If you want to play golf in an environment close to nature, then play at Southern Downs. It is a course in the true spirit of the hearty Welsh."

On the par-5 sixth hole Rosburg was one down, his second shot carried the green and in fact it ran over it, trickled up onto the fringe and then rolled back onto the putting surface and Bob had that putt for an eagle. And on the same hole Thomas drove more than 300 yards and had only an 8-iron shot left on this short par-5 hole. His ball landed safely on the green and left a 40-footer for an eagle. Dave played a fine approach putt but came up a little short and had to settle for a bird. Bob's putt looked very good but it rolled just past the cup on the left side. Both players settled for birdies and Thomas still led by a single stroke. On the par-3 seventh, Thomas had to blast his way out of a sand trap. He hit a beauty and it almost rolled into the cup and Dave settled for his par. Rosburg was faced with a 12-footer for birdie and made it. The match was now even.

On the par-4 ninth, Thomas had the honor. With the sheep grazing in the fairway, he used a 2-iron off the tee and ended up with a perfect shot down the fairway. He went on to par that hole. As some young people dressed in traditional Welsh costumes looked on, Rosburg two-putted for a par and after nine holes Thomas still led by one.

On the par-4 13th, Rosburg began to make his move. Using a 5-iron for his second, he hit a splendid shot that ran past the hole. He sank the putt for an eagle and for the first time he led in the match by one stroke because Thomas birdied. Rosburg picked up another stroke at 15 and then on 18 he beat Thomas by two strokes.

On the island of Eleuthera in the Bahamas and at its Cotton Bay Club, *Shell's Wonderful World of Golf* staged an 18-hole match between one of golf's most charismatic figures, the magnetic Arnold Palmer, and the no-less-fascinating Julius Boros. Demaret was there to do the play-by-play along with Sarazen, who described Cotton Bay like this:

"Golf on an island in the Bahamas has to do with a soft blue sky, warm breezes that rattle the coconut trees and glowing white sands seen against vivid green grass. Add to this a course designed by Robert Trent Jones, such as the Cotton Bay Club, one of his finest creations, and your world of golf becomes truly wonderful.

"A trademark of any Trent Jones layout is long tees, which allow a course to be played by golfers of every caliber. The 12th tee is close to 125 yards in length. The course has nearly 100 sprawling, big bunkers, many are set behind the greens which help to outline the target and judge an approach shot — design features I like very much. The contours of the greens are the same as the rolling sea which is always just a wedge shot away on this beautiful sunny island."

As for the match, after a strong drive on the par-5 first hole at the Cotton Bay Club, Arnie had only a 2-iron shot left to the green. And, did he rap it in classic style! The ball burned low before rising up and going all the way to the green. Arnie two-putted for a birdie on this 520-yard hole. And then Julius matched Arnie's stroke with this fine pitch-and-run third shot. Boros, too, birdied the first. At the third hole Demaret made an interesting comparison of Palmer's swing and Boros' action.

"In their takeaway, Arnie's hands, arms and club all move away with no break for the first few feet, but Boros' hands pull back first, with the clubhead following. Julius then draws the club on the inside. The clubhead then catches up with his hands as he is in a compact position on top. Arnie completes his back-swing with a big turn of his shoulders, also drawing the club on the inside, but with more extension than Julius. Arnie's thrust into the ball is what makes his action so distinctive. The right side pushes forward as he makes a big turn to the left side and like a hungry bear he slashes at the ball. But his right elbow is away from his body as he strikes the ball. In contrast, Boros works everything from the inside. His hands drop down, his left side does not turn as much and he keeps his arms close to his body. He is in an inside-out hitting position where Arnie is hitting pretty much along his line of flight. As they finish Arnie gave it that big twirl — it kind of recoils like a rifle. Julius stands upright and easy as he follows the flight of the ball. Both players drove in the fairway on this hole and went on to make routine par fours."

Arnie had a one-stroke lead after five holes and there on the sixth he was straight down the middle on this par-5 fairway. After hitting this firm wedge shot he got his par to pick up still another stroke on Boros. Palmer three-putted on the eighth green and lost a stroke, but on the ninth he had a chance to get it back and then some because Julius had a sizable putt to save par. Arnie was fooled, naturally, in trying for his birdie and it was never on line. Boros could stay close if he made his putt and with his long and smooth stroke, he did just that. Arnie led by one shot as they made the turn.

After Boros hit his tee shot within 12 feet of the cup on the par-3 15th, Palmer took his try at the special $10,000 hole-in-one prize and what an effort it was. Boros two-putted and Arnie had an eight-footer. But Palmer's wand had no magic on that day and the match remained tied after 15. At the par-5 16th, Palmer had a 2-iron second from some sandy rough and he spanked a beauty that bounced and rolled onto the putting surface. Boros missed the green with his second but his play around the greens was the key to his round. Both players got their birds and at the par-3 17th Palmer missed his birdie chance. Julius had a 12-footer for a deuce that put him a shot ahead with only a hole to play. Playing very well from tee to green through the entire match, Arnie gave it one more try at the par-4 18th. He knocked a 7-iron shot to within 15 feet of the cup but once again his putter failed him and Boros was the winner by a stroke on Eleuthera.

Two former British Open champions played the St. Andrews course on a very windy day. Britain's Henry Cotton went up against America's Sarazen. But first Sarazen described golf's most hallowed ground as follows:

"Records indicated that as far back as 1458, Scots were playing golf on this very soil. That is the Old Course at St. Andrews. Many people who come for the first time to this, the oldest and most famous of all golf courses, are often surprised. St. Andrews is not the work of some professional designer but entirely a product of nature's work. At St. Andrews, the terrain was formed as if by accident. The fairways have as much random pitch and roll as the nearby sea. Many bunkers were formed by animals digging in against wind and rain. They can be as small as the one on the 15th fairway, or as big as the famous "Hell" bunker. Among St. Andrews' most unusual features, and one seldom found on golf courses, are its double greens. Ever had a 200-foot putt?

"Many years ago, wood for new golf clubs was hung to dry in the sheds which sit at the corner of the dogleg of one of golf's most famous holes — No. 17 — the Road Hole. Just to the rear of its narrow green is a paved road and if you are on it you must play it as it lies. Many a tournament has been lost here. There is much to say about St. Andrews. It is the original golf course and remains one of the most elite. And even if you are a little disappointed at first glance, give it just a little time. Once you come to know where the hidden bunkers are or aimed at a far-off structure for the best line or how much to allow for a powerful wind, then you are beginning to understand not only the greatness of this golf course but of the game of golf itself. Many people don't realize this, but St. Andrews is a public fee golf course. All of its honored holes are open to play to one and all."

Cotton won the honor on the first tee and hit a fine drive right down the middle. Playing with his customary dispatch, Sarazen also smacked an excellent opening drive. Both hit the first green, but Cotton three-putted, and after a two-putt for Sarazen, he was one up. From the second hole through the ninth hole a sharp, northwesterly wind blew fiercely and took its toll on these two great champions. It was almost impossible to hold shots on line no matter how well they were struck. Many found the thick and wiry gorse. Even a younger generation of golfers would have been pleased to play bogey golf under such conditions. As it was, Cotton and Sarazen made the turn five- and six-over-par, respectively. Then the weather worsened. A cold pelting rain began to fall as the match reached the par-3 11th hole. But with a world of pride and the artistry that made them champions, Cotton hit the green and although Sarazen missed, both made threes. Sarazen and Cotton, both in their 60s, remained dead even as they played 16 where Sarazen ran into trouble. Gene needed a 4-wood recovery from a typical St. Andrews stance and he rose to the occasion with a club he always seemed to play so very well. Sure enough the ball reached the green and his par gave him a one-stroke lead over Cotton, who bogeyed the hole. On the 17th — the Road Hole — Sarazen hit a splendid drive around the corner of the drying sheds that have since been replaced by a hotel. One shot behind with two holes to play, Cotton aimed his drive right at the sheds and carried them easily with a mighty blow. The sun had broken through at last. The wind had abated and Sarazen boldly played with his 4-wood approach to the dangerously narrow 17th green. He drew the ball admirably from right-to-left and the ball finished on the back of the putting surface. From 60 feet away, Gene rapped an excellent putt — "a good go" as they say — and almost made a three. Sarazen took his one-stroke lead to perhaps the most famous tee in all of golf — the 18th at the Old Course. He drove down the middle. Cotton also drove well, and both hit the green with their approach shots. Sarazen two-putted for his par and Henry needed this putt to tie Gene with a 79. But it was not to be on this day and Gene won the match.

Both these historic golfing figures and the game itself were winners on that special day at St. Andrews in Scotland.

After nine years with this fabulous and unforgettable series, I became fully convinced that golf is truly the one and only universal sport and just about the only one that can be enjoyed and played by almost everyone, from cradle to grave.

The Liberty Mutual Legends of Golf

CHAPTER 3

Although the idea of *The Legends of Golf* originated from my dinner in 1963 with Gene Sarazen, I didn't realize at the time that the Shell series had another seven years of life to it. However, those intervening years between the Shell series and *The Legends of Golf* gave me time to mull it over and refine it in my mind, and also to seek counsel of the two people who would become my first two invitees — Sarazen and Demaret.

Whether we were having warm beers in Bangkok or Kuala Lumpur, my conversation with Sarazen and Demaret would invariably get around to my future golf project — *The Legends of Golf*. It traced back to the 1963 Masters when the defending champion, Arnold Palmer, was paired with the then 61 year old Sarazen. Both were tied at 147 after 36 holes of play. It was amazing that for two rounds the "Squire," whose career had spanned four decades, could still match strokes with the best players competing in the Masters. My relationship with Sarazen began with the Shell series. If it hadn't been for that association I might not have followed Gene that day, but as I sloshed around in the rain and cold, I remember thinking what a shame that all golfers, young and old, could not see this fabulous legend once more before he stopped playing competitive golf.

I don't remember the exact moment, but it was at that tournament that the thought occurred to me that television had not been around long enough to provide a record of our great champions playing in tournaments. Still, I was very much involved with the Shell series, so my dreams of *The Legends* would just have to wait.

By 1971, the Shell programs had become history. It was now time to move ahead with *The Legends*. From the very outset, I was convinced that the best format would be a four-ball tournament in which two-man teams played their best ball. I did not see this as an old-timers baseball game, but a serious, hard-fought, competitive, three-day event for a lot of money — more money than they had ever played for before.

However, with a recession gripping the country and the growing number of live PGA TOUR events on network television at that time, it began to look as though I had two chances of selling *The Legends* — slim and none – so I decided to try syndicating.

Originally, I had planned to film or tape seven matches similar to those I had produced for Shell. The matches were to include an opening round, a semifinal round and then a final round for *The Legends Championship*.

For these golfing greats who had passed the age of 50, it was most fitting to offer them their own program, *The Legends of Golf*, and to provide the opportunity to play for the largest purse in golf — $400,000.

My plan was to invite 16 golfers over 50 and pair them into eight teams. The programs would include four opening-round matches, two semifinals and the championship match. The winning team would win $100,000. Another element in this program was to be a series of clinics by these golfing greats. Not only would our cameras cover every shot played over a round of golf, but we'd also focus on course strategy. We also planned a feature where we would analyze the swings of some of the greatest players of all time — by viewing their swings both now and then.

In addition, we also intended to present special two-minute tributes to players who had died, such as Bob Jones, Francis Ouimet, Harry Vardon, Walter Hagen and Babe Didrikson Zaharias.

We would film or tape one match each day, guaranteeing maximum gallery attendance at each match, with the championship match being filmed on the seventh day of play. We were planning to tape the first two events at Demaret's course — the Onion Creek Golf Club in Austin, Texas.

The Legends of Golf was being planned as an annual event, much in the manner as *Shell's Wonderful World of Golf* and the *CBS Golf Classic*, both of which ran on television for nine years.

After many frustrating attempts to find a distribution outlet for *The Legends*, in 1977 I met with Mike Trager, NBC's Vice-President of Sports.

Mike went through the entire presentation and he liked it, but he told me if NBC bought the concept, I would not participate as a producer or director "because NBC had plenty of those around." Having been nominated for an Emmy twice and having won the coveted award once, this was a bit hard to swallow; but I was now inside the door of a major network executive who liked what he was hearing. I could not let my own ego destroy a dream I'd had for so long. Another concern was that Trager wanted a live tournament while I was worried about how the players would react to the pressure that they would be under, especially after so many years of not playing competitive golf. I put in a call to Demaret and shared my concerns.

Jimmy thought about it and then he said we should go for it. He did not think we would have any trouble getting the other players. So, I went back to Trager and told him we could deliver the players. NBC offered a one-year contract with an option for a second year. All I had to do was to go out and raise the prize money — the largest ever — $400,000. But I finally had television and it was not long before I had a sponsor — or so I thought. What we really had was a letter of understanding that said the sponsor — Nestlé —was ready to guarantee the $400,000.

The media also responded well to *The Legends* concept.

Golf Magazine wrote:

"The legends will play again — 20 golf legends will gather to compete in a record $400,000 event. Ben Hogan is expected. So is Jimmy Demaret, Sam Snead and Gene Sarazen, too. Julius Boros will be there as well as Roberto De Vicenzo and Tommy Bolt. The occasion is the first Legends of Golf *tournament to be played April 28-30 at the Onion Creek Club in Austin, Texas. Twenty of the greats from golf's*

recent past will team up in a 54-hole, best-ball medal event, and the three-day reward will exceed the career money winnings of most of the competition. NBC will televise the final two days. Total purse for the tournament is $400,000, with $100,000 going to the winning team."

Texas sports writer Jay Allen wrote:

"A couple of the legends, like Ben Hogan and Byron Nelson, won't make it, but most of the others, like Snead and Sarazen, will. The Sneads and Sarazens will certainly have help from a few others like Burke, Bolt and Middlecoff and should have no problem making The Legends of Golf *tournament live up to its name. But the players will not be the only ones with a link to the past. Male tournament officials will be dressed in knickers and old Hogan hats. Not to be outdone, the women will wear traditional ankle-length dresses."*

Jack Agnes wrote in the *Houston Post*:

"Jimmy Demaret was pushing 57 when he last played high stakes competitive golf in the 1967 Masters tournament. This was 17 years after he had won his last of three Masters titles, but he could still strike the ball as well as the young Turks and had twice as many golf shots, too. His legs simply gave out on the hilly Augusta National Golf Club course and he couldn't score well enough to survive the cut.

Jimmy thought his competitive days were behind him until a New Yorker, named Fred Raphael, sold a novel idea to the NBC television network. The event will be played at the Onion Creek Golf Club in Austin, Texas. It is one of Demaret's clubs, which means everything will be done in the best of taste. You must remember that this is the richest tournament ever conceived, and only the seniors are eligible. Twelve two-player teams will play for a purse that could underwrite the Grecian Formula concession. 'Do you realize I can finish last,' said Paul Runyan to Demaret, 'and win more money than I ever won in any tournament?' There have been reports that Ben Hogan is playing and practicing regularly at Seminole Country Club. However, Hogan hasn't committed himself to playing in The Legends. *'Hogan is a dear friend of mine,' Demaret said over a chef salad, 'but I've always contended, never let one player get bigger than the field.'"*

Hubert Mizell of the *St. Petersburg Post* wrote:

"Sam Snead killed 'em back in '49. Dominated the men's professional golf tour. Earned a whopping $31,593 which is less than half of what Tom Watson made in his first three 1978 tournaments. But there's good news, part of the good news is that Snead, if the tales are true, still has all $31,593 buried in some Maxwell House can. And the even better news is that Snead, nearing the age of 66, has a legitimate opportunity to make $50,000 in one weekend in April. Golf does more all the time to perpetuate its aging

heroes. Why, Tommy Bolt lives up the county from me and seems to make more than he did in the era when he won a U.S. Open. The ultimate of these 50 and up tournaments is one scheduled for an April 28-30 debut in Austin, Texas. It's called "The Legends of Golf" *and will present a small, select field playing for money that these guys thought existed only in Fort Knox — 400 G's — Legends, there should be a lot of them in Austin. I love the idea, and I can't wait to see those old nerves over a putt that could win $50,000 per man for some team. But even if you finish last in* The Legends, *each guy makes $10,000. At those prices, I don't look for many other withdrawals."*

Jim Trotter of *Austin American-Statesman* wrote:

"The television towers are still being installed and the press room is not finished, but preparations are virtually completed at Onion Creek for this week's Legends of Golf *tournament, an event that belies the truth that time can't be turned back. Ralph Guldahl, the slope-shouldered Texan who won the U.S. Open in 1937 and 1938, will compete. Guldahl followed his two Open victories with the 1939 Masters title, an event won over Sam Snead with one of the greatest pressure shots in golf history. Choosing a spoon (now a 3-wood) instead of a medium-length iron, Guldahl blasted from beneath a grove of trees with his second shot on Augusta's 13th hole. The ball sailed within six feet of the pin, and Guldahl eagle putted. Snead, already in the clubhouse, lost by one stroke."*

The official letter inviting the players to play was in the mail. Since all of them had agreed to play I did not anticipate any negative reaction from them. In fact, the following is a letter I sent to all the players. It is interesting that the only one I could find in my files was the one to Hogan. I guess I kept that one for sentimental reasons. If only he had accepted and played.

Mr. Ben Hogan
c/o Ben Hogan Golf Company
Box 11276
2912 West Tafford
Ft. Worth, Texas 76110

Dear Mr. Hogan:

For many of the great names in golf, television arrived a couple of decades too late. As a result, the golfing public has been deprived of the opportunity of seeing and analyzing some of the great golfers of all time, their swings and styles. But now all this will change, for beginning next year and continuing for many years to come "The Legends of Golf" *will bring together 16 "Legends" to be teamed up in a medal play partnership, best ball, two day, thirty-six hole tournament with a total prize money of $400,000 — the largest ever for any golf tournament.*

NBC has expressed great excitement over this tournament and is planning to televise it on Saturday and Sunday — May 6-7, 1978. The first tournament will be held at the Onion Creek Golf Club in Austin, Texas, and we would be honored to hold the event at your club, The Trophy Club, the following year.

The annual event will be run by the golfing participants, myself and my associates, Michael Hannan and Frank De Raffele.

Collectively, we will select the players and will be responsible for running the "Legends of Golf" tournament. The network's role will be to televise it and put up the $400,000 prize money. Checks will be given to the participants at the conclusion of play on Sunday, May 7, 1978.

We are dedicated to making this an outstanding occasion, an event which will take its place among such prestigious tournaments as the U. S. Open, the Masters and the PGA Championship.

NBC is going to provide maximum promotion for this event, unveiling their promotional campaign in January of next year and continuing up to the tournament itself.

Mr. Hogan, on behalf of my associates and myself, I would like to invite you to join us in this unusual format — which we look upon as a grateful tribute to you and the other golfing greats who will take part in this annual get-together. We would truly be honored by your participation.

Sincerely,

Fred Raphael

The players were excited. Phone calls were made as they started lining up their partners. Sarazen called me and asked if he could play with De Vicenzo. I almost cried because Julius Boros had called the day before saying that he and Roberto had agreed to play. I knew that even at 77, Gene wanted to, if not win, at least make a strong showing. He and I agreed that Doug Ford would play with him. After the first year, Doug called me and said what a pleasure it had been for him to play with Gene and he thoroughly enjoyed Gene's competitive spirit. A few years later, when Arnold Palmer joined *The Legends* and was teamed with Dow Finsterwald, those two 50 year olds were teamed up against Sarazen and his partner, Paul Runyan. As the four were introduced on the first tee, Gene leaned over to me and whispered, "Which way are you betting?"

And Gene was serious. After 10 holes the teams were tied, but then Arnold made a few birdies and it was all over.

All across the country, players who had played only a few social rounds a year were now attacking their practice ranges and playing numerous rounds of golf. I remember Demaret telling me that he must have played 100 rounds of golf to get ready for *The Legends*. Jimmy even went to Florida when the weather was bad in Houston to get in some rounds, only to run into some more rain. He finally gave up and returned to Houston.

Jackie Burke called to report that after numerous rounds he was convinced that he and partner Jay Hebert were ready to claim the first prize. And I wanted to be sure that one of my top marquee names, Sam Snead, would be near the top at the finish, so I paired him with 50-year-old Gardner Dickinson. Little did I know that Sam would spend the week carrying Gardner on his back.

Of course, the only disappointment was that Hogan would not play. But Demaret kept reminding me that no one man, not even Hogan, was bigger than the tournament ... and, of course, he was right.

We got the news that Hogan wouldn't play when he called Jimmy in Houston.

"Jimmy, I've worked on my game but it's just not fit for public display," said Hogan to his old friend. "I just wouldn't be able to help you a lick."

"Hell, Ben," Jimmy joked, "when could you ever help me?"

Despite the setback of Hogan pulling out, everything else was going as planned. What could go wrong? Plenty. On Dec. 4, with a one-paragraph letter, Nestlé informed us that it would not be able to participate in *The Legends* tournament. It wasn't going to be a very Merry Christmas, that's for sure. I knew that if I called Jimmy and all the other players they would have been very disappointed, but they would have let me off the hook. Instead, we all agreed that we would try to figure out how we could raise the prize money. Perhaps through the Pro-Am? So, we asked for a ridiculous price of $3,000 to play in a one-day Pro-Am. We then went out and got the best celebrities we could get to participate. The field included Phil Harris, Jim Garner, Mickey Mantle, Whitey Ford, Red Grange, Joe DiMaggio, Johnny Unitas, Gordie Howe, Sammy Baugh, Bob Cousy, Bobby Lane, Alan Shepard and a host of others.

As we got closer to the tournament we realized that if we sold 30 spots we would be lucky. That would have brought in about $90,000, far short of the $400,000. So we turned to NBC. I met with Trager and his lawyer and tried to find the solution to our problem. I was adamant that we would not cut back on our prize money. In retrospect, it was a mistake on my part. I should have realized that the players would have understood my position and would have played for less, but at one point in our meeting, Trager asked for time-out and left the room. When he returned, he had a plan. They would loan us the money to be repaid out of our television rights fee. They offered us the two-year contract, which included the following provisions:

If I did not come up with a sponsor in two years — to be exact by August 1, 1979 — NBC would have the right to take over the ownership of the event. Well, it was better than nothing and given two years I felt confident that I would come up with a sponsor. However, I had to admit that if it had not been for Trager — with NBC's Executive Producer Don Ohlmeyer's blessing — *The Legends* would have remained a dream and in all probability there would be no Champions Tour as we know it today.

Satisfying NBC's sponsor deadline was more of a challenge than I anticipated. Since I came up with the idea of *The Legends*, I had been desperately looking for a sponsor. While the tournament was a success after two years, I was more than $500,000 in debt and sinking fast. However, with the favorable ratings and media coverage, I was increasingly able to get in the door at a number of major corporations. For this, I shall always be thankful to Jim Hofer, who was then the advertising manager of *Fortune* magazine. I met Jim through Arthur Temple, who was a major stockholder of Time-Life and also owner of Temple

Inland and Lumberman's Investments Company, both located in Texas. Mr. Temple was very supportive of *The Legends* and steered me to Hofer. On an endless number of occasions we'd sit at Jim's desk with a sandwich and he would compile a "Who's Who" of the business world, and help set up the appointments for me.

Thanks to Jim's powerful introductions, I had no problem meeting and generating great interest among many top CEOs. My problem — and as an old advertising man, I should have known — was that when my proposal got to the agency level, some smart aleck in research would know that the cost-per-thousand for golf and its limited audience was a problem for many of their clients. I realized that just as *Shell's Wonderful World of Golf*, I needed a "rabbi" — someone to protect and advance my interests — someone like Mr. Monroe E. Spaght, who couldn't care less about ratings, etc. Spaght understood the power and prestige that golf commanded among decision makers in the business world, and just as importantly, he deeply loved the game.

Then, one morning, I was sitting at my desk (and that was really all I had) in the offices of my partner, Frank DeRaffele, when a call came in from an ad agency in Boston — Quinn & Johnson. The caller was an account executive named Eustis Walcott, Jr.

Walcott asked if I had found a sponsor for the tournament and when I told him I hadn't, he said he had one for me. I had heard that before, of course, but this time I was momentarily stunned. I had been traveling all over the country looking for a sponsor and out of the blue comes an agency I had never heard of, and an account executive whom I had never met, and they were on the verge of solving my problems. It didn't seem real.

This guy Walcott was very encouraging and he asked me to come to Boston the next morning to meet with his client. The only thing he would tell me was that they were a very conservative company — in fact, he made it a point to emphasize the word "conservative." I was to be in his office at 8:30 the next morning. I got the 7 a.m. shuttle and dressed as conservatively as I could: blue blazer, gray slacks, white shirt, red and blue striped tie and cordovan shoes. Happily, my crewcut didn't need any last-minute trim. And would you believe that with the possible change in tie, I have worn that same outfit for the past 18 years anytime I had a meeting with my "Rabbis" – although, in Walcott's case, he was probably the waspiest person I ever met.

Well, I met Walcott. He took one look at me and heaved an enormous sigh of relief with my "uniform." He said it would be just a short walk to his client's office, so off we went. As we came to Berkley Street, Walcott announced that we were just about there. As we reached the corner, my heart began to pound because directly across from me was a building with the name "John Hancock" inscribed on it. I couldn't believe my good luck! What a fabulous sponsor Hancock would make for *The Legends*. But then, as I was heading across the street, Walcott grabbed my arm, spun me around the corner, and the next thing I knew, I was being pushed into a revolving door where I was face-to-face with the bust of the Statue of Liberty and written on the wall, in the lobby of the company, was the sign: LIBERTY MUTUAL INSURANCE COMPANY. I had never heard of it.

Well, be that as it may, we were met by a secretary who ushered us into an elevator. We entered an office that was occupied by a gentleman named Jim Lynn. After the introductions were completed, Jim escorted me out of his office to another floor where I was to meet a senior executive named John Everson. Before I met Mr. Everson, Lynn suggested that I talk more to John's left side because he had a hearing problem on the right side — or was it the other way around? I was also to speak very slowly because John was into sailing and knew nothing of golf. Well, as I believe I said earlier, I must be doing something right. At first, I brought the gentleman up to date as to where the tournament stood, what I was looking for, and what it would cost them to get involved. Then I sat back and waited for the questions to come flying at me, especially about ratings, cost per thousand, etc. To my surprise, the questions went something like this: "If we wanted to talk with someone at Shell about you, whom should we call?"

I told them Hal Power. After all, Hal had been the still photographer on the series and turned out to be a great friend.

And, whom at Shell's agency, Kenyon & Eckhardt, could they call?

I suggested the senior account representative, Jim Dearborn. Jim and I had gotten along famously and were still good luncheon buddies meeting regularly at Giambelli's in New York.

And whom at J. Walter Thompson should they contact?

I suggested Buck Buchanan. Buck and I had worked together for some years and besides I was Godfather to one of his twin daughters. So, I knew I could count on Buck. Then he asked whom should they call at Filmways and the Video Tape Center? Suddenly it dawned on me that these three gentlemen weren't focusing on the tournament, but me. They were trying to determine what kind of a guy they were dealing with. And since Lynn kept bouncing up and down like a yo-yo, rushing to the nearest telephone, I guessed that by the time the interview ended they knew as much about me — businesswise — as I knew myself.

Soon, it was time for lunch. I had been there about three hours. I didn't want to get cocky, but I was beginning to feel optimistic. We headed for my first luncheon at the Algonquin Club, an experience that I'm most happy to report has been duplicated many, many times since.

I knew they were serious when they started asking questions about NBC and my contract with the network. Then came a bombshell, the likes of which I will never forget. Evenson told me that they wanted to be the sole sponsor of *The Legends*. In other words, they wanted to buy all the advertising time for the show. I told them that the networks and agencies had clients who wanted to be associated with a number of golf projects so I didn't think buying out 100 percent of the show would fly, but I was sure that NBC would be most happy to sell 50 percent to Liberty and in that way, Liberty could "control" the project and have their names associated with it. I truly couldn't believe what I was hearing. Wait until Bert Zeldin, head of sales at NBC, got wind of what I was hearing from Liberty. Not since the good old Shell days had I met a client who wanted to own all the time on its show.

The lunch concluded and the Liberty Mutual executives asked that I give them first refusal rights on *The Legends* for a period of two weeks. Apparently the chairman of Liberty Mutual, Melvin C. Bradshaw, was out of the country and would be back in Boston by that time. I didn't know it at the time, but Mr. Bradshaw was going to be my new Mr. Spaght.

Down the road, I found out that Julius Boros was a member of the Liberty Mutual sports staff and a very close friend of Mel's. Julius, knowing how desperate I was to find a sponsor, had practically pre-sold Mel on the idea of Liberty's sponsoring what would be renamed *The Liberty Mutual Legends of Golf.*

As we left the Algonquin, the Liberty Mutual team headed back to its offices on Berkley Street and I headed to Logan Airport. At this point, Evenson looked at me and said, "Look, we've been interrogating you all day. Here's a copy of our latest annual report, it should give you a pretty good idea as to who we are." Now, reading and understanding annual reports is not my strong point, but I noticed toward the end of the report that the company, then under the name of Massachusetts Employment and Insurance Association, went into business in 1912 because of a law that provided for the establishment of a private insurance company to carry out the Workmen's Compensation Act. Now, why they went into business didn't catch my attention, but the year 1912 did because that was the year that Ben Hogan, Sam Snead and Byron Nelson were born. Thus, 1912 would be, for me, a year to remember.

I couldn't wait to get to the office the next morning to place a call to Bert Zeldin at NBC. At this point, let me remind you that my original contract with the network stipulated that in order to get the loans from NBC, which contributed greatly to the prize money in 1978 and 1979, I had to agree that if I did not have a sponsor sealed, signed and delivered by August 1, 1979, NBC had the right to take over ownership of *The Legends.* It was now the middle of June 1979 and I was definitely running out of time. Also, since I was out there doing the selling, I had to come up with a sponsor who had never been in golf. In other words, I had to put "new" money on the table. That's why Liberty Mutual proved to be such a coup.

It was now between 8 and 8:30 a.m. and, fortunately for me, Zeldin had pretty much the same habits as I did. I reached Bert and said, "I believe I have a sponsor and they would like to purchase at least 50 percent of the commercial time in *The Legends*," There was silence on the other end of the phone for what seemed like an eternity. Finally Bert said, "OK, Fred, who is it?" I said quietly, "Liberty Mutual Insurance Company from Boston."

"Liberty who?" Bert asked. Two weeks later, on July 17, 1979, to be exact, I received a telegram from Jim Lynn confirming their willingness to sponsor what would come to be known as *The Liberty Mutual Legends of Golf Tournament*.

NBC arrived early the week of the inaugural tournament, led by producer Larry Cirillo. Larry and I became extremely good friends. *The Legends*, right from the beginning, became Larry's favorite golf tournament. We would sit for hours in Capriccio's Restaurant or Mora Manadie's in New York City planning and creating new ideas for the tournament and the telecast.

Larry worked extremely hard on *The Legends* and as a way of showing my gratitude for his effort and our friendship, I always tried to get him a good pairing in the Pro-Am. One year I paired him with Sam Snead, which scared Larry to death. He struggled for the first 13 holes or so and finally, when they came to the 15th tee, Sam took Larry aside.

"Larry, I'm going to show you how to play golf," Sam said.

Snead proceeded to change Larry's stance and grip and told him to step up and hit that ball.

"That's it?" Larry asked.

"That's it," Snead said. "Just follow through."

Larry went on to par the next three holes and then birdied the 18th.

"Now you're a golfer," Snead said as they walked off the last green.

In our first year, Larry took advantage of old black and white footage to come up with an opening for *The Legends* that was original and different from other golf programs. Using the music of the 1930s and '40s for background, he created an opening montage that included just about all of *The Legends*. It was a great introduction to the show.

We agreed that the program would lend itself to interesting quizzes about the history of the game.

FOR EXAMPLE:
Video Audio
Shot of Sarazen, Snead, De Vicenzo, Thomson and Nagle.
All of these five Legends won the British Open.
Question: **Who was the oldest of this group at the time he won the Open?**
Answer: Roberto De Vicenzo was 44 years old, plus 93 days when he won at Hoylake in 1967.

Cut to shot of De Vicenzo.

Shot of Sarazen, Boros, Guldahl and Middlecoff.

All five of these Legends won the U.S. Open.

Question: **Who was the youngest of this group at the time he won the Open?**

Answer: Gene Sarazen was only 20 when he won his first U.S. Open in 1922, at the Skokie Country Club.

Cut to shot of Gene Sarazen.

Shots of Ryder Cup, etc.

This competition between the U.S. and Great Britain for the Ryder Cup began in 1927. It was not until 1937 that the U.S. team won the cup on British soil.

Question: **Since then, how many times has the British team won the Ryder Cup?**

Answer: The matches were not held during World War II. Since 1947 through 1977, a period of 30 years, the British team had never won any of the matches played either in the United States or in Great Britain.

Cut to shots of Worsham, Snead, Guldahl, Runyan and Bolt.
One of these five Legends won two consecutive U.S. Opens and three Western Opens in 1936, 1937 and 1938.

Question: **Who was it?**

Answer: Ralph Guldahl won the U.S. Open in 1937 at Oakland Hills and in 1938. He won his three con-secutive Western Opens in 1936 at the Davenport Country Club, at the Canterbury Golf Course in

1937 and he defeated Sam Snead at the Westwood Country Club in 1938.

Video – cut to Guldahl.
Shots of Sarazen, Bolt, Demaret, Burke and Boros.
Which one of these Legends won all four major championships — The U.S. and British Opens, the PGA and Masters.
Question: **Who was it?**
Answer: Sarazen is one of four professionals who accomplished this achievement and he was the first to win all four titles. The others were Ben Hogan, Jack Nicklaus and Gary Player (since joined by Tiger Woods).

Video – cut to Sarazen.
Shots of Demaret, Snead, Ford, Burke and Middlecoff.
Question: **Which of these Legends was the first golfer to win the coveted Masters title three times?**
Answer: If you said Jimmy Demaret, you are right. Jimmy did it in 1940, 1947 and 1950.

Video – cut to shot of Demaret.

Of course, it was only fitting that I write to Joe Dey of the USGA and ask him to send me a letter to be posted on the bulletin board describing Rule #41, Fourball Stroke Play. Back came the following from Dey:

RULE #41 - FOURBALL STROKE PLAY

"The Legends of Golf tournament will be played under the rules as approved by the United States Golf Association and the Royal and Ancient Golf Club of St. Andrews, Scotland. The format will consist of Fourball Stroke Play. In Fourball Stroke Play, two competitors play as partners, each playing his own ball. The lower score of the partner is the score of the hole. If one partner fails to complete play of a hole, there is no penalty."

And, in keeping up with the tradition of *The Legends*, we encouraged our NBC announcers to refer to the clubs used by the players as their old names, such as spoon, cleek, mashie, niblick, etc.

From the moment that my press release went out, I announced that I would be inviting one player who was not yet 50. Of course, that one Legend had to be Arnold Palmer. But Arnold couldn't play. When the press at Onion Creek cornered Peter Thomson about being 48, they wondered how he got invited. I reminded them that, from the very beginning, I would be inviting one player who was not 50, yes — and that player was Australia's Peter Thomson. In truth, I didn't realize Peter wasn't 50, but everyone seemed to buy my story about Peter's invitation.

Our tournament director, Bob Rule, was hand-picked by Demaret and we could not have made a better choice. Bob had run tournaments in Texas, including at Champions. He was a fine gentleman and his contributions were one of the reasons we had such a great tournament. Bob was optimistic — a trait that I was running short of at that time — and I needed Bob because I had never run a tournament before. Despite the fact that we had a small gallery, the event still broke even. Either Bob used mirrors or he had a "fairy godmother" he never told me about.

The sweetest words I ever heard from Bob came in 1980 when he called and said, "Fred, I just heard from Doc Giffin. Arnold Palmer will play in *The Legends*."

After Rule came a man who was to be the best tournament director I've ever had the pleasure to know and to work with, Bill Bass. A retired executive from the Armour Co., Bill and his wife lived on the first tee at Onion Creek. In fact, if memory serves me right, Bill built the second home on the Onion Creek property.

Jimmy once described both Rule and Bass as two of the most honest, talented and caring people he ever knew and he was right. It was interesting that in the years that they ran the event it never lost money. And everyone, including our sponsor, Liberty Mutual, and their guests left the tournament very happy and with fond memories of a wonderful week with *The Legends*.

To really get in the mood to enjoy the story of the *The Liberty Mutual Legends of Golf Tournament*, a two-man team tournament, you would have to start in the locker room at the Onion Creek Club on Tuesday, April 25, 1978. That's when I truly realized for the first time that the tournament wasn't going to be like any other tournament that I had ever been part of.

Tommy Bolt, more famous for throwing clubs than winning the 1958 U.S. Open, was sitting over in another corner telling a reporter one of his favorite stories.

"I came to the 18th hole in one tournament after hitting a gorgeous tee shot about 260 yards straight up the fairway," said Bolt. "I left myself about 125 yards to the green. I studied my shot for a moment then asked my caddie, 'Boy, what do I need for the shot?' My caddie replied, 'It's a 5-iron.' 'Boy, you're crazy, I only have 125 yards left.' 'Yes sir, I know that,' the caddie replied. 'But you don't have anything but a 5-iron left, either.'"

"You know I've been told that my putter had more airtime than Lindbergh, and I guess that's right," Bolt said. "When I let it fly everyone knew 'Ol' Tom' was around. But I remember Ky Laffoon once had a bad week with his putter and he tied it to the rear of his car and dragged it all the way to the next tournament. It was nothing serious. He just wanted to punish it a little."

Jay Hebert was asked if he ever drew any bad caddies during his playing days.

"Did I ever draw any bad caddies?" he moaned in mock seriousness. "Let me tell you about a wino that caddied for me in Arizona one year. He was about 45 years old, stood string straight and was looking at the world through terribly bloodshot eyes. Everything went along well for about four holes, but on the fifth, we were playing into the sun and I hit a tee shot and couldn't even see the ball.

"I turned to my caddie and asked, "Where did it go?' My caddie looked at me and blandly said, 'Where did what go?' Yes, I have had a few bad caddies in my time."

A writer asked Dr. Cary Middlecoff if he was always as intense as he appeared to be on the golf course.

"Well, I'd say I'm very even-tempered," said Middlecoff. "I'm mad all the time."

I remember Doc being very excited to come to Austin to visit with so many of his old friends, but he was more than a little nervous about putting his game on public display, since it had been quite a long time since the former U.S. Open and Masters champion had played competitively. Still, it didn't take long for Demaret to help him relax. Early in the week Jimmy saw him in the locker room and said, "Doc, what the hell are you thinking about? You made millions playing golf and now you're going to blow it all on a comeback?"

Sarazen probably made very sound investments in his career, but he was still eager for his share of the prize money. "I can't believe we're playing for $400,000!" he said. "In 1932 when I won both the U.S. Open and British Open I got less than $1,000 for winning both championships. In 1935, I got $750 for winning the Masters in a playoff with Craig Wood. By the way, Craig and I each got an extra $50 for playing 36 holes in that playoff."

Demaret, listening to Sarazen, said, "Hell Gene, when I won the Masters in 1940 I got a check for $900. Last year they gave me $1,000 just for showing up at the Champions Dinner!"

"Lighthorse" Harry Cooper, an Englishman who grew up in Dallas and twice won the Canadian Open and was leading money winner on the tour in 1937, joined in.

"Heck, I was leading money winner in 1937," he said. "I won seven tournaments for a total of $14,138. They get more than that for finishing about third today. Of course, don't forget that we didn't pay taxes in those days."

Sam Snead also strolled down Memory Lane.

"Before I became a pro I used to be a soda jerk in my home town, Hot Springs, Va." Sam said. "The old Doc who owned the shop would go out and look around, and as long as one person was on the street, he wouldn't close up. We didn't have traffic lights in my town. As a matter of fact, we only had one stop sign. Well, nothing in my home town has ever changed. One weekend Jimmy Demaret came by to play an exhibition with me. He said, 'Hey Sambo, it is Saturday night. Where's the action around here?' I said, 'Well Jimmy, we can go down and watch 'em get a couple of haircuts,' " Snead continued.

"I was the leading money winner in 1949 and 1950 and if the purses had been what they are now, I would have made about $400,000 each year," said Sam, who won 11 tournaments in 1949 and earned only $31,593. "The purses don't bother me because I was just out there to win tournaments. Like Leo Durocher said, 'You show me a good loser and I will show you a seldom winner.' People who say you play the course and not the other players — that is a bunch of hokey. You play the same guy you're playing against. You've got to have the killer instinct. When you got 'em down, kick 'em."

Sam wasn't kidding, either. As Middlecoff said at the time, a lot of fellas were just in Austin for a good time, but Sam was like a kid with his first set of clubs. I think it was more than that, though. Sam was the most competitive player I ever saw in all my years around the game.

I'll give you the perfect example: In the 1982 *Liberty Mutual Legends*, Sam was paired with Don January, who was 17 years younger than Sam and just joining the Senior PGA Tour. I guess you could say they were a pretty strong team since in 54 holes Sam made 14 birdies and Don made 13. They never bogeyed a par 3 and played them in 10 under par. They were nine under on the par 4s and eight under on the par 5s. They led by a stroke after the first round and by eight after the second round. They could have phoned it in from there, but Sam went out and played like everything he owned was on the line. After he birdied the 15th and 16th holes, January asked him, "Man, how much do you want to win by?"

"You never know," Sam said. "Those folks up there ahead of us might be cheating."

For the record, Snead and January won by 12 strokes.

Sam said he once went 13 straight years without being away from golf for more than two weeks in a row. He even took an African safari in 1965 during that streak to get away from the pressures. Even there, he was talked into an exhibition match in Nairobi and had to play in a pair of Hush Puppies. He broke even against the country's best amateurs and won three leopard skins.

In his late 60s at this point, Snead was realistic about his game.

"I'm a senior player now and not a helluva good one at that," he said. "I'll get one thing cured and something else will break out. It's like an old car. You put in new bushings and the pistons go. You fix the pistons and the brakes fail on you.

"I made my swing as simple as possible. That way, you have less to go off," he said. "You want a swing that can stand up under heat and pressure. When a player blows up, it's not necessarily because he choked. He loses his concentration. That's

Jack Nicklaus' biggest asset — his power of concentration. Nothing bothers him."

A reporter interviewed Ralph Guldahl about his career, which included wins in the 1937 and 1938 U.S. Opens and the 1939 Masters. Guldahl claimed that a shot he played on the 13th hole at Augusta in '39 to overtake Snead should be compared with Gene Sarazen's famous double eagle at Augusta in 1935.

According to Guldahl, on the par-5 13th hole, he slipped on the rain-soaked tee and hit a short tee shot down the left side of the fairway. The safest shot would have been to lay back short of the creek which ran in front of the green. At that time there was high brush behind the green but he decided to gamble and pulled out his 3-wood. It had to be kept extremely low for the first 75 yards, and he brought it off by toeing the club in and hitting sharply down on the ball. The shot came off perfectly, flying under the tree branches and stopping six feet from the pin. Guldahl knocked in the putt for an eagle and went on to beat Snead by one stroke.

Jimmy Demaret went on to recall how he had once turned down a job as a professional singer.

"It paid $1,500 and that was a lot more than I was making playing golf, but golf was my love, so I just sang for my own amusement," Demaret explained.

Although he managed to make a fine living from golf, Snead recalled that he preferred playing baseball during his boyhood. "I thought I was going to be a professional baseball pitcher until I threw my arm out," Snead recalled. "Let's see, I played pitcher, catcher, shortstop — every position except first base. We used to play in these coal mining towns, and we would have to carry baseball bats with us wherever we went because those coal miners would just want to fight, so we'd take our bats along and say, 'Hey buster, if you want it, come and get it.'

When asked about his hometown, Sam kept the press in stitches.

"It hasn't grown at all," Sam said. "Every time somebody is born, somebody either dies or leaves town. We have four or five new houses, but at least four or five have burned down, so the old town is just about holding its own."

Reporter Melanie Hauser asked Sarazen how much longer he would play competitive golf.

"I don't know, this could be my last year or next year could," Sarazen said. "It all depends on how I feel. When you get to this age, how you play depends on your mood." Gene played for another 10 years at *The Legends*.

"Because of television," Gene said, "there's a lot of money in the game. It's real big business now. Television made golf what it is today. In fact, it made all sports what they are. We played for peanuts compared to what they play for today. But a dollar isn't worth as much now. They have an awful lot of them, though. They really enjoy their gravy train."

Everything at this point was coming up roses for *The Legends of Golf.* The players couldn't be happier. The press was very supportive, as was NBC. But it wouldn't be a golf tournament without a few near disasters or a misunderstanding or two.

Back in 1978, almost all the players stayed at the Crest Hotel, located alongside the Colorado River on First Street. The stories were plentiful as they gathered together, night after night. We had two social evenings that year, and Tuesday was our evening to introduce the players and those legends of all sports who had been invited to participate in the Pro-Am on Wednesday.

Every year we had a big dinner and one of the most memorable was the year we honored the late Harvey Penick, who was already a legend in his own right in Austin before his best-selling *Little Red Book* was ever published. My plan was to have Harvey introduced by two of his favorite pupils, Ben Crenshaw and Tom Kite, whom he loved like they were his own sons. That was the plan, at least, but it almost resulted in a great embarrassment for me and *The Legends*.

It seems that while my people had contacted Ben, no one had gotten in touch with Tom. Fortunately, on the morning of the dinner, a writer friend of mine ran into Kite. After visiting for a while, he told Tom he'd see him at dinner that night. Tom, who was obviously hurt, said he hadn't been invited. When I learned this, I immediately called Tom, apologized for the screw-up, and pleaded with him to join Ben in introducing Mr. Penick. Happily, Tom agreed and he and his wife, Christy, came to the dinner. The introduction Ben and Tom gave Mr. Penick was one of the most moving and heartfelt I've ever heard, and there were more than a few tears shed among those at the dinner — a dinner that had grown so large that we held it at the University of Texas fieldhouse.

There was one more concern to deal with before we could celebrate a successful debut. Our entertainment that night was the local grammar school band, led by their teacher, a lovely lady whose name is a distant memory to me now. Included in our list of celebrities was the famous Broadway and Hollywood star, Gordon MacRae. Jimmy Demaret was anxious for Gordon to entertain. The only problem was that Gordon wanted $1,000 to sing a few songs from "Oklahoma" — and he wanted to be paid before he sang. I did not have that kind of money on me so we pooled the money from friends at the banquet. Then the real fun began.

Gordon and the youngsters could not get together on anything. It was a scene right out of an old Mack Sennet movie. MacRae then tried singing with just the accompaniment of the piano player. That didn't work, either. I thought for sure that Gordon would not perform and we'd get our money back. Suddenly Gordon announced that he would sing without any accompaniment. He did perform very well, and, yes, he kept the $1,000.

Then there was PGA TOUR Commissioner Deane Beman. Not long after the first *Legends* wrapped up, I got a phone call from then Commissioner Beman. Some stories were written here at the conclusion of the tournament that had caught his eye. He said he wasn't demanding equal space, he just wanted to set the record straight.

In the first place, Beman wanted to go on record as not being against tournaments for the older generation.

"Senior events are a part of our policy and will continue to be," he said. "I personally enjoy them. I think they add interest to the game. I thought *The Legends* went very well."

What Beman said he did not like about *The Legends* was that most of the money came from NBC.

"From what I understand there was no organization in Austin that sponsored *The Legends* similar to the Houston Golf

Association co-sponsoring the Houston Open with the PGA," said Beman. "It was put on by one-man: you."

Beman had been criticized for predicting that the two amateurs in the field, Dale Morey and Bill Hyndman, would win. Bill became ill at the last moment and Ed Tutwiler substituted for him.

"Let me explain that situation," said the commissioner. "During the Tournament of Champions I was in the locker room and we were discussing *The Legends*. I said there might be a surprise — that the amateurs might fool some people and win it. At the time I said that, I thought Hyndman was playing. The reason I said it was because I knew Morey and Hyndman have been playing a lot of golf and are competitively sharp, whereas most of the players in *The Legends* had not been playing competitively."

I told him that his information regarding NBC's underwriting the tournament for a $1 million was not correct. What they did guarantee was that they would cover any money that would be short in covering the purse. I believe we sold about $90,000 for the Pro-Am, so NBC had to loan us $310,000.

However, in order to secure that loan, I had to repay it out of my two-year contract…$200,000 each year, and if I did not come up with a sponsor by April 1, 1979, NBC would take the tournament away from me. A rather stiff price, but I had no other way of raising the prize money.

Ultimately this would be water under the bridge. What I will never forget from that first morning is walking out of the locker room at Onion Creek down to the practice area. There they were: Sarazen, Snead, Demaret, Middlecoff, Runyan, Thomson,

De Vicenzo, Boros — so many great players who had become my friends. It was a dream of 15 years that had come true. I really did not care who noticed that my eyes were filling up with tears. As Bob Toski said when he saw the 76 year-old Sarazen birdie the par-5 18th hole, "I never knew crying felt so good."

It was now noon on Friday and it was only fitting that Sarazen lead *The Legends* off the first tee. Gene, as usual, wasted little time once he had his ball teed up and, as usual, drove it right down the middle.

The Legends of 1978 were on their way.

At the end of the day, the Australian team of Peter Thomson and Kel Nagle had taken the lead with a six-under-par 64, a one-shot lead over Snead and Gardner Dickinson. Thomson and Nagle, the favorites to win this inaugural event, had won the World Cup twice and were runners-up in that tournament a couple of times as well.

Surprisingly, Toski, now one of the most heralded teaching pros in the world, and former PGA champion Chick Harbert were two strokes back at 66.

For his part, Sarazen made a four-footer for a birdie on No. 12 and drew a lot of praise from Toski, who was playing in the same group.

"All he's lost is the length off the tee, but he's still got the shots," Toski said. "He's a great inspiration to play with."

Toski is one of my favorites. Because of his small stature, he had been the brunt of many jokes over the years by his fellow pros. Demaret once said Bob was "the only guy he knew of who needed a lifeguard to take a shower." Snead said, "If Bob had a tail, cats would chase him. Dave Marr once tried to rake a trap with him and Middlecoff once threatened to use Mouse — as Toski was called — as a ball marker."

The second round was important, not only to the players, but to NBC and myself as well. It was to be our first day on television, but there was one catch: We had to wait until a game between the Cincinnati Reds and the New York Mets was completed. We were scheduled to go on the air at 4 p.m. EST, but the game seemed to go on forever. Finally, the game came to an end about 45 minutes late, and our *Legends* finally made it onto network television — and did those guys put on a show!

My old friend, Sarazen, didn't disappoint any of us as he birdied three holes on television and later told the press: "I'll be here at 80!"

And he was.

But the day really belonged to Snead. Sam made six birdies that afternoon, and with no ropes to keep him away from the galleries, Sam was practically being mobbed as he walked down the fairways. We permitted the galleries to roam about onto the fairways with their legends, just as they did years ago. Of course, when Arnold Palmer joined *The Liberty Mutual Legends of Golf* in 1980, we had to rope off the course or we would never have finished a round of golf.

But getting back to Snead, as we all knew, Sam may have had just about the perfect golf swing. Not only did it look perfect, but it also worked perfectly, producing one pure drive after another. His putting style was a different matter. Despite his unorthodox putting style, Sam did make all those birdies and he and his teammate, Dickinson, shot an eight-under-par 62 and took the lead after 36 holes of play. They were 13- under-par with a score of 127.

"I putted better and I guess I played better, except on the last hole," said Sam. "I used up all of Texas on the last hole. It went right to right, then right again." This drew a good laugh from the press. "Overall, I was very pleased with the way I hit the ball today."

At the end of their press interview, Sam looked at his partner and said, "Gardner, now go home and please get lots of sleep."

Gardner was an ideal partner for Sam in that first *Legends*. They were both no-nonsense characters on the golf course, and they had teamed well in the old CBS Golf Classic, winning in 1967. One reason for their success was Gardner was a very reliable player, so he would usually hit first off the tee figuring that he would usually hit the fairway or the green, allowing Sam a chance to turn on the power or try to tuck it in close to the hole on the par 3s. There was another reason as well: Gardner honestly respected Sam and made it known that Sam knew how much Gardner respected his ability. But he wasn't a sycophant, by any means. He'd give Sam the needle every now and then to keep him loose. But he did show Sam the respect he deserved and Sam always responded well to that.

There was one problem, though, and it produced a funny exchange between the two late in the final round.

Gardner liked to hit the ball hard, especially under pressure when, as he said, "trying to get cute will kill you."

They came to the 17th hole, an uphill par 3 of about 145 yards. Gardner hit first and his ball came to rest about 20 feet left of the hole. Sam, who was looking for an edge, asked Gardner what he hit. Gardner told him he hit a 9-iron. Sam was incredulous.

"Dammit, Gardner, I'm your partner," Sam said. "Now what did you really hit?"

Gardner showed Sam his 9-iron and Sam shook his head in disbelief. He went back to his bag, changed clubs twice and finally played a beautiful little cut shot that nearly went in the hole. As they walked off the tee, Sam turned to Gardner, showed him the 5-iron he'd hit, and gave Gardner that famous Cheshire cat smile of his.

Sunday, Snead did it again. He and Gardner shot a closing four-under-par 66 for a total of 17-under-par 193 to edge Thomson and Nagle by a single stroke.

Playing in the final group, the two teams came down to the last hole at 16 under. Thomson's approach flew over the green. Nagle faced a 20-footer for birdie. Dickinson had a 15-footer but Sam was just two feet from the hole after hitting a beautiful sand wedge from 73 yards for his third shot. When Nagle left his birdie putt 10 inches short of the hole, Jackie Burke exclaimed, "Short! I can't believe it. I'd have had to chip it back to hole if I missed it!"

That left it up to either Snead or Dickinson to sink the winning putt or face a sudden-death playoff. Sam putted first and never had an easier putt for $50,000.

When Sam's putt disappeared into the cup, Mike Souchak said, "Gardner better go give him a great big hug and a kiss!"

And why not? Over 54 holes, Snead made 14 of the team's 18 birdies. They bogeyed just one hole. Dickinson had been treated to one of the greatest 54-hole shows ever put on by a 66-year-old. On his own ball, Sam would have defeated the entire field with the exception of Thomson and Nagle. Sam was like a young kid at Christmas time. He was excited and thrilled by his play.

"The first 36 holes I hit my irons as good as I could hit 'em and this was my best putting since I was forced into my side-saddle style several years ago."

Witness what Sam did with his putter:

On 13, he holed a five-footer to save par and stay within a stroke of the Australian team. On 15, he sank an eight-footer and his team remained one stroke behind the leaders. On 16, he canned a 12-foot birdie to remain one shot behind after Nagle made a 13-footer. On 17, he knocked in a nine-footer for a birdie to tie the Aussies and then on 18, he brought home the bacon with the winning birdie putt.

"I felt when I made the birdie at the 17th hole, we could win it with a birdie on 18," Sam said. "Then when Nagle missed his chance at the 18th, I said, 'Well, looka here,' and I knew it was ours."

Everyone made out well that last day.

Paul Runyan and Lew Worsham finished last with three-over-par 213 and split $20,000. Just as he predicted, Paul's share was more money than he had won as the leading money winner on the PGA TOUR in 1934.

One of my favorite stories from that year concerned Doc Middlecoff and his partner, Bob Rosburg. While Doc hadn't played much, Rossie had kept his game in pretty good shape, and I kind of thought that if Doc could get on a streak early, they might be an interesting team to watch. Unfortunately, Doc struggled and finally, just as they made the turn in the final round, Rossie came up with a brainstorm.

"Doc," Rossie said as they left the ninth green, "why don't you go in the clubhouse and get yourself a drink."

Doc thought that was a pretty good idea and, in fact, it turned out to be just that. Doc birdied Nos. 10, 11, and 13 and Rossie added a birdie at No. 12 as they went on to win the biggest check of Doc's career.

And so, the initial *Legends of Golf* was history.

Speculation now turned to whether *The Legends* would return to Onion Creek — or move on. I had been quoted as saying that there was only a 50 percent chance that *The Legends* would return to Austin. I was told that major companies like 3M and Western Corp. were interested in coming in as sponsors and moving *The Legends* to another location. I received a call from someone connected with the Hilton Hotel in Las Vegas who wanted me to take the tournament there.

But I was thinking about the tremendous work and loyalty of our wonderful volunteers at Onion Creek. They were really responsible for making the tournament a success. The gallery for a first-time event proved to be more than satisfactory and Demaret wanted me to stay in Austin and, specifically, at Onion Creek. What convinced me to stay was something Sarazen told me when we were having a farewell drink at the Crest Hotel that Sunday night.

"Fred," he said, "Augusta became well-known around the world because of the Masters. Some day, people will say Austin is the home of *The Legends*."

As usual, the Squire knew how to cut right to the core of the situation.

In the pressroom the event was considered a huge success by everyone and, very importantly, NBC executives concurred. It was now the first week in May and *Sports Illustrated* was on the streets. One of its finest writers, Dan Jenkins, had been at *The Legends of Golf* and he wrote:

> *"At first it was like packing up a golf museum and taking it on the road. In fact, a lot of folks out there thought Arnold Palmer had invented the game and then lost it to Jack Nicklaus at one of those places like Pensacola or Pinehurst. If so,* The Legends of Golf *would show them different. Ben Hogan's white cap and cigarette might be missing, but on display would be such treasured relics as Gene Sarazen's knickers, Sam Snead's straw hat, Tommy Bolt's chin, Jimmy Demaret's wit, Cary Middlecoff's dental drill and all sorts of memorabilia from the sport that gave us beltless slacks and three-toned shoes."*

The sportswriter Oscar Fraley, author of *The Untouchables*, added:

> *"The fellow who said life begins at 40 must have been so near-sighted he needed a seeing-eye dog. Tack on 10 years and you had a fantastic life beginning for all our senior professional golfers. Without a doubt,* The Liberty Mutual Legends of Golf *was the tournament that provided a rebirth for the greatest names in golf.*

"The year was 1978, when The Legends *was planned to be a one- or two-year reunion for a bevy of Demaret's rockingchair pals.*

"But when Sam Snead thrilled a national TV audience with a birdie barrage for victory and when an even larger TV audience watched Julius Boros and Roberto De Vicenzo defeat Art Wall and his playing partner, Tommy Bolt, in a six-hole playoff a year later, a pop-eyed nation realized these golfing gaffers still could play a helluva game."

The Day The Champions Tour Was Born

APRIL 29, 1979

CHAPTER 4

With our inaugural year behind us, we were ready to tackle 1979. Added to the field were Art Wall, Freddie Haas, Dick Mayer, Jerry Barber, Bob Hamilton, Walter Burkemo, Bob Goalby, George Fazio and Ireland's popular Christy O'Connor — "Himself," as he was known in his homeland. Staying with our original concept of inviting two top amateurs, we included two outstanding golfing generals, John Compton and John Kline. The message from our tournament director said it all when he headlined his letter greeting our volunteers, "It was Great in '78, and it will be Super Fine in '79. Little did Bob or anyone else have any idea of the spectacular finish, one of the greatest in golf, that was about to unfold before us that year.

The letter said:

> *"The inaugural* Legends of Golf *tournament played at Onion Creek Club in 1978 resulted in priceless international exposure for the club and for the City of Austin.*
>
> *"The fact that the tournament is returning again in 1979 is ample evidence that the players, the creator of the tournament and the executives of NBC were completely satisfied with the hospitality and diligent work of the Onion Creek members. Many other cities were considered before the decision was reached to return* The Legends *to Onion Creek. But the players found the course very much to their liking, and almost to a man they expressed a desire to return. This was a strong factor in the decision to bring the tournament back in 1979. Undeniably, the creator of the tournament, Fred Raphael, would like to see Onion Creek become a permanent home for the event, which should increase in stature every year as new Legends such as Arnold Palmer, Billy Casper, Don January and others become eligible to compete.*
>
> *"This will be the critical year.*
>
> *"A smashingly successful tournament in 1979 will not only be encouraging to our friends from New York, but it will strengthen the desire of Onion Creek officials to bring the tournament back year after year."*

A clue to what would happen at our second *Legends* tournament took place the moment play began on Friday. In order to keep one of my biggest names in prominence, I asked 50-year-old Bob Goalby, then an NBC announcer, to play with then-77-year-old Gene Sarazen. I had seen enough of Gene's play in 1978 to realize that the Squire, despite his age, could still play an amazing round of golf. His burning desire to win was still there. Whoever made the remark "that while there may be snow on the rooftop there was still a fire burning in the belly" must have had Gene in mind.

On Saturday, I was up in the clubhouse with about 100 members watching the tournament on television. The opening of the show was followed by NBC cutting to the scoreboard to update the viewers and for a moment my heart stood still and tears rolled down my cheeks when announcer John Brodie exclaimed, "And look who are in second place, just one shot off the lead — Gene Sarazen and his teammate, Bob Goalby." Gene not only had great talent as a golfer, but he also had the uncanny knack of making headlines.

And now, here was Gene, with a good chance to win.

I had paired Gene with my friend, Bob, because I thought Bob's game might keep them near the top of the leader board and because I knew Bob could handle Gene's personality, which could get a little testy at times. Naturally, Bob was thrilled and excited to play with Gene — a pairing of Masters champions.

As I mentioned, they made the turn right in the thick of things, just as I had hoped. On the 12th hole, Gene hit his ball into a hazard and picked up, putting all the pressure on Bob, who hit a good drive and a great approach shot that left him with a tricky putt for a birdie. Bob really worked hard on that putt and when he made it, he couldn't wait to get back to see Sarazen, who was resting in his golf cart, to get his reaction.

"What'd you make on that hole, partner?" asked Gene.

Years later, Bob still laughs about that.

While they didn't win, that opening to our Saturday telecast helped set the tone for what was to follow for the rest of that day and to the spectacular finish which would take place on Sunday — a day none of us associated with *The Legends* will ever forget.

I had gone to bed on Saturday confident that we had a great telecast that could bring solid ratings, proving that 1978's ratings were no fluke. The players were proving yet again that they could still play exciting, competitive golf.

But around 3 a.m. I was rudely awakened by an enormous thunderstorm — one the likes of which I had never seen. I became very nervous since a rainout was the last thing we needed, especially since we were in a position to capture a good share of the television audience on Sunday. The good news was that NBC had a pre-recorded show scheduled just ahead of us, which meant that we would not be up against the possibility of a delay in our 4 p.m. EST telecast. (Remember, I was hoping that a potential sponsor might be out there watching on Sunday.) I knew the storm was heavy out there, but we still had 7½ hours before the first tee time.

Still, the storm and the stress it produced made sleep impossible, so I dressed and drove through the storm to Onion Creek. Once I got there, my worst fears were confirmed. The course resembled nearby Lake Travis. About an hour later NBC's Larry Cirillo arrived. There was little we could do but shake our heads, drink more coffee and, of course, pray. We were joined by Bob Rule, then Terry McGovern who ran the pro shop, and finally, the chief of our ground crew, Jack Treece. Despite their moral support there was little we could do but wait. It wasn't quite daylight, but every time we left the locker room to see what was happening outside, it became increasingly obvious that getting in a round of golf was going to be difficult, if not impossible.

Around 7:30 a.m. the phone began ringing. First the media called, then the galleries, and finally the players. Some of our players were beginning to check the airlines to arrange for an early departure. All we could do was to ask everyone to stand by as we checked with all our weather sources. The weather was so bad I finally called the hotel and suggested that my wife make reservations to fly back to New York. She did, and as a result she missed out on one of the greatest playoffs in golf history.

About 9:00 a.m., a member of Onion Creek came into the locker room and announced that he'd been in touch with the Breckenridge Air Force Base outside Austin and had some encouraging news. The Air Force anticipated that the heavy rains would stop in about an hour and we could expect clearing weather for the remainder of the day. That was the good news. The bad news was that we faced an enormous challenge in getting the course in playing condition.

At this point we turned to Treece. He started making phone calls. He ordered all the sand he could locate in Austin. Then the call went out to club members and other local golf course grounds staff to come to Onion Creek and help with what proved to be a massive cleanup job.

At about 10 a.m. the rain ceased and Jack and his crew went to work. In the meantime, Harold Sargent, our head official, met with Cirillo and myself and we agreed to split the field, starting half off the first hole and the other half at the 10th hole — then unprecedented on the PGA TOUR. While the rains stopped, the skies remained threatening and gray for the rest of the day and, of course, the soft fairways didn't give the players much roll, although at 6,300 yards, not much was needed. However, rain-soaked greens did give the players an opportunity to attack the pins and once play began birdies were everywhere.

The weather almost caused another potential problem as well. Roberto De Vicenzo was staying with some friends and we had no way to contact him. It wasn't until 30 minutes before his tee time that Roberto showed up in the locker room to pick up his equipment. He had assumed the round was canceled.

So, despite the gray and overcast skies, we kept our fingers crossed. Rather than my trying to put down on paper what happened that day, I'll turn that task over to sports writer Denne Freeman, who wrote the following column 10 years after that memorable playoff took place.

"Yes it was strictly this stuff of Legends. When Julius Boros' partner, Roberto De Vicenzo, was sinking his fifth consecutive birdie in a six-hole sudden-death shoot-out to defeat Tommy Bolt and Art Wall, A.C. Nielsen reported that viewers in almost 6,000,000 homes had caught up to and stayed with the most dramatic and exciting conclusion of a golf match ever seen on television. Over and above golf's

normally measured appeal in TV homes, there were the millions of viewers who packed locker rooms and gathered around clubhouse and saloon television sets to watch a sudden-death playoff that would go down in golf history. The Legends of Golf, in just its second year, was fast earning a reputation for legendary finishes."

One funny thing about that playoff was that as well as all the guys played, Roberto wound up winning the playoff after hitting his drive into the wrong fairway. Later, in the locker room, Tommy Bolt joked that while he didn't mind losing, it bothered the hell out of him to lose to a guy who couldn't even drive it onto the right hole, never mind the fairway. Over the years, Bolt and De Vicenzo would always joke about that.

Even though I didn't realize it at the time, Sunday, April 29, 1979, should go down as the day the Champions Tour was born.

After the tournament ended, I went back to the locker room. By now, it was almost empty. The staff was busy cleaning up and an attendant told me none of the players had left until the playoff was over. Most of them had even changed their flights. I learned later that the excitement in that room had been unbelievable. What a shame we didn't have a camera in there. It would have made historic television coverage.

I don't think that I fully realized the impact the tournament had until I went into Mike Manuche's Restaurant on 52nd Street in New York for lunch the next day. As I sat at the bar, I began to hear people asking their drinking partners, "Did you see that unbelievable finish at *The Legends of Golf* on television yesterday?"

Everyone in the place seemed to be talking about it. Sports agent Eddie Elias, sitting over in a corner, gave me a "V" sign — the Churchill victory salute. I called NBC, but Larry Cirillo wasn't around. I wanted him to join me and experience the excitement *The Legends* playoff had created. If this was a sample of what was happening around the country, then *The Legends* would soon have a sponsor and senior golf was here to stay.

In the days to follow, the media took over. The letters from the players and the golfing public were more than I ever could have anticipated.

From the media came these reports:

"Go on, you mean you didn't see it? You missed that shoot-out in Texas?

"What were you watching on television, arm wrestling from Grenoble? Hockey? First man down court shoots, or what? Not The Legends of Golf? *Well, if you have a minute or so I'll try to tell you what happened, but it just might defy description. I mean, even the television folks were speechless at times over what happened. What it was was one of the greatest shows on earth."*

— *Dick Taylor,* **Golf World**

"Anyone who tuned in to The Legends of Golf *show late must have thought they were seeing excerpts from the best shots ever made on* Shell's Wonderful World of Golf.*"*

— *John Brodie,* **NBC Telecaster**

"On an Onion Creek course that tested more than strength, the foursome of De Vicenzo and Boros and Wall and Bolt put on an exhibition of golf, matching shot for shot on the first five playoff holes and making the tournament worthy of its name."

— **Bill Sullivan, Austin American-Statesman**

"Adrenaline that for years had come with leaky faucet speed was rushing in torrents. The gray, paunchy ones were suddenly thrust back into time. They were young again. They were in the hunt again. This was The Legends of Golf, *and the teams of De Vicenzo and Boros, Wall and Bolt showed why they were invited — in spades. They finished the 54 holes tied at 195, 15 under par. And away they went into a sudden death playoff that will go down in golf history. Heck, it may become legendary."*

— **Bob Galt, Dallas Times Herald**

"At age two, it's almost a Legend! If you were fortunate you watched The Legends *during Sunday's six-hole playoff. It was the first truly Legendary playoff. The future of the tournament is solid. It scored well in television ratings a year ago, probably scored higher this time, surely will leap again next spring because anyone who viewed the play-off will not soon forget it. All in all,* The Legends of Golf, *is the finest thing to happen to the city of Austin since the invention of the enchilada."*
— **Fran Boggs, The Daily Oklahoman**

From NBC Sports:

Back in New York, from NBC headquarters came the following announcements as The Legends *kept playing "follow the leader," hole after hole:*

3:45 PM   *Be sure to stay tuned to watch Sportsworld at the conclusion of* The Legends of Golf.

4:30 PM   *Remember, Sportsworld will follow the conclusion of* The Legends of Golf.

5:30 PM   *Sportsworld will not be seen tonight so that we may bring you the conclusion of* The Legends of Golf.

6:10 PM   *The local news will be seen immediately following the conclusion of* The Legends of Golf.

6:25 PM   *The local nightly news will not be seen tonight. Stay tuned for our network news following the conclusion of* The Legends of Golf.

6:50 PM   *The Sunday night network news will not be seen tonight so that we may bring you the conclusion of* The Legends of Golf.

NBC:

"In two days, The Legends *was seen on television for a total of seven hours, including 4 1/2 hours on Sunday. The response to the program from viewers all over the country was unanimous in praise of the event, the quality of play, the excitement, fun and good fellowship displayed by the players — and all were delighted that we stayed with it to its spectacular conclusion."*

—Bert Zeldin, Vice President NBC Sports Sales

From *The Legends of Golf*:

"This means as much to me as winning the U.S. Open. After all, I'm not competing with the younger boys anymore and this, The Legends of Golf, *is a new and exciting challenge to me. My daughter just called me from my club and said it was a 'standing room only' gang in the clubhouse and all ordering drinks — on me!"*
— **Julius Boros**

"In all of my fifty years of golf, I have never seen anything to equal this finish. NBC should have had a camera in the locker room. No one left until it was over. Most missed their planes. Everyone was cheering and shouting — it was like Super Bowl Sunday. This is one of the happiest and most exciting moments of my golfing career and I think George Fazio and I finished next to last — or we should have."
— **Jimmy Demaret**

"It was truly a fantastic finish. But playing here in The Legends *is one of the greatest thrills — if not the greatest I've ever had."*
— **Art Wall**

"Not since my double-eagle in the Masters have I enjoyed anything more than The Legends of Golf. *I thought I had retired at 70. Now I want to play in* The Legends *until I'm 80!"*
— **Gene Sarazen**

And from the public:

"Your Legends of Golf telecast was one of the best ever. Maybe it was because I can better relate to Bolt, Boros, Wall, De Vicenzo, Burke and the like, yet at the same time you had all the elements of a terrific show — excitement, outstanding golf, fun and fellowship displayed by the players. It was the best golf show I have ever seen on television."
— **W.R.Y., Executive Secretary,**
Bob Hope Desert Classic, Rancho Mirage, Calif.

"Just wish to thank and congratulate you for televising the second Legends of Golf this past weekend. As an older golfer who has followed the former greats in tournaments over the past 30 years, it was wonderful to see them play again, under tough competitive conditions." — **C.C., Canton, Maine**

"I have watched a lot of golf and television but I have never seen anything as good as The Legends last Sunday. WOW! What a format." — **C.C., Spokane, Washington**

"Thanks for showing The Legends of Golf. It was refreshing to view the program and to see how well the 'old ones' do. Please stage this show again next year.

"As a long time-golf enthusiast, I can only say that your presentation of The Legends of Golf produced one of the most thrilling moments which I have ever witnessed in the history of the sport." — **Eugenia Velez, New York, N.Y.**

"Coverage of The Legends *was the most enjoyable in memory. At 52, I especially liked old favorites still playing magnificent golf. I can hardly wait 'til next year."*

— **H.E. Harrington, North Carolina**

Unfortunately, not every NBC affiliate covered the playoff — including, of all places, the Austin affiliate. At 3:30 p.m. the plug was pulled on *The Legends* broadcast at the Dallas microwave switching center, just when a putt by Roberto De Vicenzo was rolling toward the cup on the 17th hole.

Apparently more than a month prior to the tournament, KTTV contracted with the Copenhagen and Skoal people to air the Rodeo Superstar Classic instead of NBC's Sportsworld, which was scheduled to follow *The Legends of Golf.*

Austinites fortunate enough to have cable were able to switch to San Antonio's KMOL and were able to follow *The Legends* to its conclusion, which didn't come until a little before 7 p.m. EST. What added to the dramatic impact was the nine birdies that the "over the hill" gang had out of 12 possible scores on the extra holes. Mike Campbell, general chairman of *The Legends* tournament, said, "I missed the whole playoff. I had to get checks made out for the other teams. I thought they might want to leave, but they weren't leaving the locker room. They were like a bunch of kids. They would just go nuts, jumping up and cheering. They were having a helluva time."

Three golf-related events happened in 1980 that were to permanently change the future of *The Liberty Mutual Legends of Golf* and golf for players 50 and over. First of all, *The Legends,*

130

now firmly established as an artistic success, became a very solid financial success with the strong support of our newly found sponsor, the Liberty Mutual Insurance Company. Second, the formation of the Senior PGA Tour — now the Champions Tour — in effect, an outgrowth of *The Legends* tournament, and third, the appearance of Arnold Palmer, who turned 50 and accepted an invitation to play in *The Liberty Mutual Legends of Golf* and whose participation on the Senior PGA Tour made it a certifiable success.

It goes without saying but it is worth repeating that without the support of Liberty Mutual, *The Legends of Golf* would never have succeeded and golf's greatest mulligan would never have been born. As I pointed out, they found me. That's an important point I'll never forget, and neither should all the players on the Champions Tour.

The deeper I got into Liberty Mutual's history, the more I realized that the company and *The Legends* were made for each other.

In 1980, the King, Arnold Palmer, turned 50 and joined *The Legends*, and so did his "army." Approximately 100,000 golf enthusiasts crammed every nook and cranny of Onion Creek that week. Other newcomers included Arnold's playing partner, Dow Finsterwald, Dan Sikes, Jack Fleck, Bobby Hamilton, Chandler Harper, Ted Kroll, George Bayer, Ed Furgol, Walter Burkemo, Harry Cooper, Jim Ferrier and Don January. Arnold's agreeing to play in *The Legends* was crucial, not only for *The Legends*, but for senior golf as well. Besides, here I was with a new sponsor and what better way to welcome them to *The Legends* than announcing that one of the greatest legends of them all would be with us in Austin the following spring. However, getting Arnold did present me with one problem. Arnold, in a letter to me, indicated that he wanted to play with his old buddy, Dow Finsterwald. I wondered about that pairing — putting two 50-year-old players together seemed a bit unfair to the rest of the field. I was in a quandary. There was no way I wanted to turn down Arnold. I might lose him and that would be disastrous for me, the tournament and my new sponsor. So, I put in a call to Jimmy Demaret and explained my dilemma. Jimmy thought for a minute, and more than likely had another swig of his beer, and said, "Fred, let them play together. Hell, they're not going to win." I agreed. I had now set a precedent that would haunt me from that day on. Forever more, when two players who were friends turned 50 and qualified, they invariably wanted to be partners in the tournament. They wouldn't hear of being paired with a player in his 60s, or even late 50s. But I had a precedent and I had to live with it through the years.

However, a pair of 50-year-olds never have won in their first year of *The Legends*. Good old Jimmy — he always came up with the right answer, or at least, one that made sense. In the 17 years since Palmer turned 50, he only missed one *Liberty Mutual Legends of Golf* event. And other than the first year when there was correspondence between us, I would usually write to Arnold about dates, etc., and there would be no further correspondence between us. But he was always there ready to play.

He missed the 1997 event because the tour scheduled the Bay Hill Classic — Arnold's regular PGA TOUR event — head-to-head against *The Legends*. At the time, I attended the Ronald

Reagan Awards Dinner in which Arnold was honored at the prestigious Jonathon Club in Los Angeles. As I arrived at the banquet, I joined the reception line and as I approached Arnold, the first thing he said to me was, "I can't play in your tournament next year. They've put my tournament against yours."

Golf has never had a greater ambassador representing the game than Arnold Palmer. He is charismatic, unselfish with the galleries and even his fellow players appreciate what he has done for golf.

At the dinner, I was flattered to be asked to say a few words. What I remember most was that I ended by saying, that on behalf of all my fellow senior sponsors, that I wanted Arnold to know that we respected him, admired him, but most of all we loved him.

Arnie's Army was in its glory. A man named George Embright was a happy man. He came all the way from Springfield, Missouri to attend *The Liberty Mutual Legends of Golf* and finally obtained Palmer's autograph.

"I can't believe it," the retired Army master sergeant exclaimed, looking at Palmer's signature scrawled on his tournament program, "This is better than any Christmas present I ever got. It's even better than when I got out of the Army."

Embright said he first began trying to get Palmer's autograph at the Western Open in Cleveland in 1964 but couldn't fight his way through the crowd to get to Palmer. After that, he said, he experienced a seemingly endless series of frustrations as he sought the coveted autograph.

"I had just about every other big name player's autograph," Embright said.

"I figured there wouldn't be as many people here as in the PGA (TOUR) tournaments. Boy, was I surprised at the crowds, but I decided to wait just outside the clubhouse. When he came out I shoved the program in his face and he signed it. I couldn't believe it was so easy." Embright says that he planned to frame the program and hang it over his fireplace in his den.

Others were not so fortunate. While standing next to the green on the first hole, Issie Pistalk, who was on vacation in the Austin area from Helene, Ontario, blew her chance for a memorable picture. Palmer was lining up a putt when an adventuresome squirrel ran from a nearby tree and raced between Palmer and the ball. Pistalk had the shot lined up but froze and didn't snap the shutter. Pistalk was philosophical about her missed opportunity.

"I only have one frame left and I wanted to get Palmer while he was putting," she said. "Besides, I came all the way from Montana to see Palmer and I'm not going to take a picture of a squirrel. We have squirrels in Montana. Do you think I'm going to waste film on a squirrel?"

Among the souvenir hunters, John Agan, 13, a Round Rock, Texas, eighth grader, was better organized.

"I got a lot of autographs," Agan said. "I got Palmer, Demaret, Larry Gatlin and that media guy, Schenkel or whatever his name is." It was Chris Schenkel, the ABC sports commentator.

Even the simplest thing Palmer did pleased his adoring fans.

"He's going to walk, he's going to walk. He's nice looking," a woman excitedly exclaimed to a friend as Palmer opted to walk down the fairway instead of riding a golf cart. "He's the King. He's the King, isn't he? He's the King." Said Jim Schroeder, a beer distributor from Lockhart, after watching a Palmer shot, "In modern days of golf, he's been the big source, the starting point. Jack Nicklaus is up there with him, but Palmer started it."

The Beginning of the
Champions Tour

CHAPTER 5

But 1980 would prove to be a most important year for golf, especially the seniors, because the Champions Tour got off the ground with two events in addition to *The Liberty Mutual Legends of Golf*. The Champions Tour, which would become the success story of the '80s laid the groundwork for its development at a meeting at the PGA TOUR's headquarters on January 16, 1980.

Attending that meeting were Sam Snead, Julius Boros, Gardner Dickinson, Bob Goalby, Don January and the late Dan Sikes. Sikes, a former lawyer, was named honorary chairman.

At that meeting it was recognized that the strength and

attraction of a senior tour hinged on the reputations made by the players over their playing years on the PGA TOUR. At first, the fields were limited to 50 players and the eligibility criteria concentrated on a player's position on the Career Money List and his number of career victories.

In order for their events to be a financial success, the players agreed that two of the three rounds of play would include playing with amateurs. One of the Pro-Am rounds became an official round of the tournament.

Two tournaments were held that year — one in Atlantic City, New Jersey, and the second, the Suntree Classic, in Melbourne, Florida. The purse for the Atlantic City event was $125,000 and was won by Don January with a score of 208, five under par.

The Suntree Classic also had a purse of $125,000. Charlie Sifford was the winner and collected $20,000 for his triumph. January, who had won the Atlantic City tournament, finished four strokes behind Sifford in second place.

As the Senior PGA TOUR grew to 10 events, I was having lunch with one of the players in New York. During the course of the luncheon, he told me about a proposal the players had received from a company in Denver which indicated that a major airline wanted to take over the senior tour. What caught the attention of the players was that this firm was making a commitment to add $100,000 to each of the current events then on the tour. Most events were averaging about $125,000 a tournament and to add $100,000 to the purse for each of the existing events was something the players naturally wanted to explore.

The player I was having lunch with asked me if I would meet with this group and report back to him as to whether or not these fellows were sincere or just blowing smoke. I agreed to look into it and I flew to Denver to meet with the airline's public relations agency. They were certainly sincere in their wanting to increase the purses and of taking over the tour, but their bubble burst when I asked how they planned to raise $1 million to cover the increase in purses. Their answer was "through television." They planned to buy time from ESPN and then sell commercials to advertisers to raise the money. Their sponsor would guarantee the $1 million to cover 10 events.

They were confident that they could sell all their advertising for $30,000 a commercial. I couldn't believe what I was hearing, $30,000 for a spot on ESPN? I knew the cost of commercial time on the networks for golf and the $30,000 was what the broadcast networks were looking for from advertisers. At ESPN, the going rate was $3,000 a spot, not $30,000. Somebody seemed to have added a zero into these figures. I knew my numbers were right because we had just gotten Liberty Mutual to sponsor a promotional program on ESPN for *The Legends* called *Liberty Mutual Legendary World of Golf* and the cost was $3,000.

When I pointed this out to the group before me, silence fell over the room. The president of the airline had another meeting to attend and the PR guys were dumbfounded. The meeting came to a rapid conclusion and I was on my way back to New York.

I advised the players that there was no way that this group could put together the package that had been described to them. And, for what it was worth, I strongly suggested that they leave all TV matters and organization to the PGA TOUR. The TOUR, under the leadership of Beman, was slow in its start of supporting the seniors, but Beman was now 100% behind it. I felt the success of the Senior Tour was tied to the PGA TOUR and not some outside group expressing an interest in it. Unfortunately for the airline, they went out of business in less than a year after expressing an interest in taking over sponsorship of the Senior Tour.

At just about that time I heard from Commissioner Beman. He asked me to meet him at a PGA TOUR event just outside Washington, D.C. We met at his hotel room and with him was Labron Harris, another member of the TOUR staff. The Commissioner confirmed that there would be a Senior Tour and they were inviting *The Legends* to join them. Since *The Legends* had been so successful and I had a network contract, it would help the new Tour immensely. I remember him saying that *The Legends* joining this new Tour would help them both now and that someday down the line, I might need their help. I thought it was a good idea. In fact, I was most anxious to be a part of anything that might be good for the over-50 gang. All I was hearing was that I wasn't as crazy as many people thought. As I had hoped, predicted and prayed for, there were lots of people out there who would come out and support the over-50 players.

Nothing further came of our conversation until about a year later, when a young man from South Africa, now working with the seniors, visited me at my desk.

I still had just a desk. Nothing had changed financially for me since NBC still had my rights fee money.

Brian Henning, better known to the golf world as Bruno,

was there to invite *The Liberty Mutual Legends of Golf* to join the Senior Tour. I liked Bruno and I told him, on behalf of *The Legends*, I would like very much to be part of what would become the Senior PGA TOUR. Bruno left my office a very happy man. In his position as executive director of the Senior Tour, he had contributed greatly to the success of the new venture. My respect and admiration for him is such that in 1997 I honored Bruno by presenting him with "The Jimmy Demaret Award" at our tournament.

What I did not realize at the time was that because of our team-play format and because we were an invitational event, we would be classified as an "unofficial" event. This meant that any money that players won in our event would not count as part of their official earnings. Back then the "unofficial" tag did not mean much, due to the fact that there were not many events on the Senior Tour. With no more than 10 or even 15 events, all the players looked forward to playing in every event they could enter and *The Liberty Mutual Legends of Golf*, with the largest purse on the Senior Tour at that time, always attracted the very best senior players.

The two who immediately come to mind were Mickey Wright and Kathy Whitworth. The problem was that neither was 50. However, I had been told that the senior age for women was 45, so I proceeded to invite them. Once the invitations went out, one would have thought that I had started World War III. I caught hell from everyone. And it didn't help when after the first round of play Mickey and Kathy shot a 65 and were in fourth place. They cooled off after that and ended up in the middle of the field. Perhaps if I had paired them with male legends, it would have met with the approval, but to have them compete with the boys was a no-no. I even had them playing from the men's tees, but it didn't make a difference.

However, I never lost sight that this was first and foremost an event that was created for television and thanks to the presence of Mickey and Kathy, we scored the highest Nielsen ratings to date for our tournament — except for the six-hole playoff in 1979.

Wright and Whitworth were the gallery's favorites, especially after the first round. They fell back to a 72 in the second round and finished with 69s. The rain-softened course didn't help the shorter-hitting women. It was a fact that the men pros didn't exactly cheer the presence of Mickey and Kathy, but I believe these two ladies had all the credentials to belong in the tournament. In fact, they were probably more legitimate *"Legends"* than some of the men who teed off that week.

They proved to be champions who had done it all and were delighted just to be in Austin. When I called Mickey to invite her, she was thrilled and practiced daily. After all, she hadn't played much competitive golf in years while Kathy had been playing on a regular basis with the LPGA. Also, the guys weren't particularly happy that I had invited Kathy, who was 45 and not 50, the required age for male seniors. When the press questioned me about Kathy's age, I simply replied that I didn't believe it was gentlemanly of me or any other male to inquire as to a woman's age.

Although his team's play would have been better, Palmer found other ways to keep his Army happy. On the seventh tee, an elderly Austinite was standing nearby when Arnold, saying nothing, quietly slipped his golf ball into the surprised old man's hand as he walked up to the tee box.

"I imagine that's one he'll be hanging onto for a long time," chuckled the gentleman's son. And he added of Palmer, "That man's a truly great Legend."

Amen. I'm just glad that one of my legacies is that golf fans — young and old alike — will enjoy the play of my "*Legends*" for years to come.

Looking back on my years in a game I knew nothing about, I'm thankful I've had such a great run. I couldn't have asked for anything better.

SHELL'S WONDERFUL WORLD OF GOLF MATCHES
1962-2002

2003   FRED COUPLES VS. MICHAEL CAMPBELL

Matauri Bay, Northland, New Zealand . . . . .Kauri Cliffs Golf Club

2002   PHIL MICHELSON VS. DAVID TOMS

Homosassa, Florida . . . . .World Woods Golf Club

FRED COUPLES VS. MARK CALCAVECCHIA

Czimel, California . . . . .Preserve Golf Club

2001   SAM TORRANCE VS. CURTIS STRANGE

Portsmouth, Rhode Island . . . . Carnegie Abbey Club

PHIL MICKELSON VS. SERGIO GARCIA

Los Cabos, Mexico . . . . The Club at Querencia

CRAIG STADLER VS. SHIGEKI MARUYAMA

Tokyo, Japan . . . . .TPC at Ichihara

KARRIE WEBB VS. ANNIKA SORENSTAM

Las Vegas, Nevada . . . . Las Vegas Painte Golf Resort

JACK NICKLAUS VS. BEN CRENSHAW

Santa Fe, New Mexico . . . . Las Campanas

JACK NICKLAUS VS. ARNOLD PALMER

St. Augustine, Florida . . . . King and Bear

2000   DAVID DUVAL VS. ERNIE ELS

Charleston, South Carolina . . . . Cherokee Plantation

NOTAY BEGAY III VS. HAL SUTTON

Rose Hall, Jamaica . . . . .White Witch

PAUL AZINGER VS. JESPER PARNEVIK

Gulfport, Mississippi .... Grand Bear

FRED COUPLES VS. PHIL MICKELSON

Oklahoma City, Oklahoma .... Gaillardia

JACK NICKLAUS VS. GARY PLAYER

London, England .... Sunningdale

1999 NICK PRICE VS. ERNIE ELS

Mpumalanga, South Africa .... Leopard Creek

JIM FURYK VS. COLIN MONTGOMERIE

Paris, France .... Paris Golf Club

DOTTIE PEPPER VS. KARRIE WEBB

Hanover, Ohio .... Longaberger Golf Club

FRED COUPLES VS. JOHN DALY

Sunriver, Oregon .... Crosswater

HALE IRWIN VS. TOM WATSON

Princeton, New Jersey .... TPC Jasna Polana

1998 TOM LEHMAN VS. PHIL MICKELSON

Bay Harbour, Michigan .... Bay Harbour Golf Club

FRED COUPLES VS. ERNIE ELS

Whistler, British Columbia .... Nicklaus North

PAYNE STEWART VS. NICK PRICE

Aruba .... Tierra del Sol

JUSTIN LEONARD VS. DAVIS LOVE III

Mamaroneck, New York ....Winged Foot

GARY PLAYER VS. LEE TREVINO

St. Augustine, Florida, World Golf Village – The Slammer and The Squire

1997 TOM LEHMAN VS. NICK FALDO

Barbados .... Royal Westmorland

TOM KITE VS. SEVE BALLESTEROS

Cantabriz, Spain . . . . Royal Pedrena

FRED COUPLES VS. TOM WATSON

Kilkenny, Ireland . . . . Mount Juliet Golf Club

PHIL MICKELSON VS. COLIN MONTGOMERIE

Vail, Colorado . . . . Cordillera Club

JACK NICKLAUS VS. JOHNNY MILLER

San Francisco, California . . . . Olympic Club

1996   ARNOLD PALMER VS. GARY PLAYER

Lanai, Hawaii . . . . The Challenge at Manele

JACK NICKLAUS VS. LEE TREVINO

Cabo San Lucas, Mexico . . . . Cabo del Sol

ANNIKA SORENSTAM VS. DOTTIE PEPPER

Kiawah Island, South Carolina . . . . Kiawah Island Resort

GREG NORMAN VS. FRED COUPLES

Sutherland, Scotland . . . . Skibo Castle

TOM KITE VS. BEN CRENSHAW

Houston, Texas . . . . Champions Golf Club

1995   GREG NORMAN VS. NICK PRICE

Hobe Sound, Florida . . . . The Medalist Club

JACK NICKLAUS VS. TOM WATSON

Pebble Beach, California . . . . Pebble Beach

CHI CHI RODRIGUEZ VS. LEE TREVINO

Humucao, Puerto Rico . . . . Palmas del Mar

PHIL MICKELSON VS. ERNIE ELS

Tenerife, Canary Islands . . . . Golf del Sur

PAUL AZINGER VS. SEVE BALLESTEROS

St. Andrews, Scotland. . . . . Old Course at St. Andrews

1994   RAY FLOYD VS. FRED COUPLES

La Romana, Dominican Republic .... Casa de Campo

ARNOLD PALMER VS. JACK NICKLAUS

Pinehurst, North Carolina .... Pinehurst #2

GREG NORMAN VS. NICK FALDO

Berkshire, England .... Sunningdale Golf Club

1970   ROBERTO DE VICENZO VS. TOM WEISKOPF VS. DAVE STOCKTON

Buenos Aires, Argentina .... Ranelogh Golf Club

BOB MURPHY VS. DAN SIKES, JR. VS. MILLER BARBER

Mount Irvine, Tobago .... Tobago Golf Club

LEE ELDER VS. GEORGE KNUDSON VS. GEORGE ARCHER

Sao Paulo, Brazil .... Sao Fernando Golf Club

JULIUS BOROS VS. FRANK BEARD VS. LEE TREVINO

Mexico City, Mexico .... Club de Golf Bellevista

GEORGE KNUDSON VS. ROBERTO DE VICENZO

Winnipeg, Canada .... St. Charles Country Club

FRANK BEARD VS. DAN SIKES, JR.

New Orleans, Louisiana .... New Orleans Country Club

DAN SIKES, JR. VS. ROBERTO DE VICENZO

San Francisco, California .... The Olympic Club

1969   BEN ARDA VS. BILLY CASPER VS. GENE LITTLER

Manilla, Phillipines .... Manila Golf & Country Club

ARNOLD PALMER VS. GAY BREWER VS. CHI CHI RODRIGUEZ

Fajardo, Puerto Rico .... El Conquistador Hotel & Club

ROBERT DE VICENZO VS. BERT YANCEY VS. TONY JACKLIN

Nairobi, Kenya .... Karen Country Club

DOUG SANDERS VS. CHARLES SIFFORD VS. DAVE THOMAS

    Singapore .... Singapore Island

DAN SIKES VS. AL GEIBERGER VS. PETER ALLISS

    Kamuela, Hawaii .... Mauna Kee Beach Hotel Golf Club

FRANK BEARD VS. GARDNER DICKINSON VS. JULIUS BOROS

    Kingston, Jamaica .... Caymanes Golf & Country Club

FRANK BEARD VS. DOUG SANDERS VS. ARNOLD PALMER

    Palm Beach, Florida .... PGA National Golf Club East Course

BEN ARDA VS. ROBERTO DE VICENZO VS. DAN SIKES

    Ontario, Canada .... London Hunt & Country Club

FRANK BEARD VS. BEN ARDA

    Medinah, Illinois .... Medinah Country Club #3 Course

SANDRA HAYNIE VS. CAROL MANN VS. KATHY WHITWORTH

    Bangkok, Thailand .... The Royal Bangkok Sports Club

1968   MASON RUDOLPH VS. GARDNER DICKINSON

    Guatemala City, Guatemala .... Guatemala Country Club

PHIL ROGERS VS. DAVE THOMAS

    St. Andrews, Scotland .... Old Course at St. Andrews

FRANK BEARD VS. SEBASTIAN MIGUEL

    El Prat, Spain .... Real Club de Golf

DON JANUARY VS. CHRISTY O'CONNOR

    Newcastle, Northern Ireland .... Royal Country Down

JULIUS BOROS VS. ARNOLD PALMER

    Eleuthera, Bahamas .... Cotton Bay Country Club

DOUG SANDERS VS. PETER ALLISS

    Portugal .... Perina Golf Club

SANDRA HAYNIE VS. CAROL MANN

    Vaud, Switzerland .... Lausanne Golf Club

BILLY CASPER VS. GAY BREWER

Miami, Florida . . . . Doral Country Club

AL GEIBERGER VS. GEORGE KNUDSON

Victoria, Canada . . . . Oak Bay Golf Club

ROBERTO DE VICENZO VS. SAM SNEAD

Washington, District of Columbia . . . . Congressional Golf Club

1967   BRUCE DEVLIN VS. TOMMY JACOBS

Rome, Italy . . . . Golf Club of Rome

PETER ALLIS VS. TONY LEMA

Bermuda . . . . Mid-Ocean Golf Club

ANTONIO CERDA VS. JOHNNY POTT

Mexico City, Mexico . . . . Golf Club of Mexico

PETER THOMSON VS. DAVE MARR

Holland . . . . Golf Club "de Pen"

MARLENE STREIT VS. MICKEY WRIGHT

Mississauga, Canada . . . . Toronto Golf Club

MIGUEL SALA VS. BILL CASPER

Caracas, Venezuela . . . . Lagunita Country Club

JEAN GARALAIDE VS. KEN VENTURI

Versailles, France . . . . La Boulie Golf Club

JULIUS BOROS VS. SAM SNEAD

Atlanta, Georgia . . . . Peachtree Golf Club

DAVE THOMAS VS. BOB ROSBURG

Brigend, Wales . . . . Southerndown Golf Club

HAROLD HENNING VS. DOUG SANDERS

Hesse, Germany . . . . Frankfurter Golf Club

ROBERTO DE VICENZO VS. TOM WEISKOPF

Morocco . . . . Fedala Golf Club

1966 TONY LEMA VS. ROBERTO DE VICENZO

Athens, Greece .... Glyfada Golf Club

MIKE SOUCHAK VS. CHI CHI RODRIGUEZ

Canal Zone .... Panama Country Club

MARLENE STREIT VS. MARILYNN SMITH

Oslo, Norway .... Oslo Golf Klubb

BILLY CASPER VS. DOUG SANDERS

Brookline, Massachusetts .... The Country Club

BRUCE DEVLIN VS. CHARLES SIFFORD

Malaysia .... Selangor Golf Club

GENE LITTLER VS. GEORGE KNUDSON

Ottowa, Canada .... Ottawa Country Club

RAMON SARA VS. BOBBY NICHOLS

Madrid, Spain .... Club de Campo

SAM SNEAD VS. JIMMY DEMARET

Colorado Springs, Colorado .... Air Force Academy

GEORGE WILL VS. DAVE MARR

Ayrshire, Scotland .... Turnberry Golf Club

BEN ARDA VS. DOW FINSTERWALD

Rizal, Phillippines .... Valley Country Club

CHEN CHING-PO VS. TOMMY JACOBS

Osako, Japan .... Iberaki Country Club

1965 DAVE MARR VS. BERNARD HUNT

London, England .... Sunningdale Golf Club

TONY LEMA VS. CARL POULSEN

Ruhgsted Kyst, Denmark .... Rungsted Golf Klubb

JAY HEBERT VS. FRIEDEL SCHMADERER

Lower Saxony, Germany .... Hamburg Golf Club

CHI CHI RODRIGUEZ VS. TOMMY JACOBS

Nassau, Bahamas .... Lyford Cay Club

BEN HOGAN VS. SAM SNEAD

Houston, Texas .... Houston Golf Course

GEORGE KNUDSON VS. AL BALDING

Nova Scotia, Canada .... Cape Breton Highlands

JOE CARR VS. AL GEIBERGER

County Kerry, Ireland .... Killarney Golf Club

JOHNNY POTT VS. ROBERTO DE VICENZO

Zulia, Venezuela .... Maracaibo Country Club

PHIL RODGERS VS. ALFONSO ANGELINI

Lombardia, Italy .... Villa d'Este Golf Club

MARLEY SPEARMAN VS. MARILYNN SMITH

Luxembourg .... Luxembourg Golf Club

BARBARA ROMACK VS. ISA GOLDSCHMID

Monaco .... Monte Carlo Golf Course

1964 JULIUS BOROS VS. MIGUEL SALA

Bogota, Colombia .... Country Club de Bogota

MICKEY WRIGHT VS. BRIGETTE VARANGOT

Portugal .... Estoria

DAVE MARR VS. FLORY VAN DONCK

Brussels, Belgium .... Royal Golf Course

GEORGE KNUDSON VS. STAN LEONARD

Vancouver, Canada .... Capilano West

TONY LEMA VS. CHEN CHING-PO

Shizuoka,Japan .... Fuji, Kawana

DOUG SANDERS VS. CHI CHI RODRIGUEZ

Dorado, Puerto Rico .... Dorado Beach

BOBBY NICHOLS VS. JACKY BONVIN

Valais, Switzerland . . . . Cransa-Sur-Sierre

DAVE RAGAN VS. BOB CHARLES

Maui, Hawaii . . . . Maui

JOHNNY POTT VS. KEL NAGLE

New Delhi, India . . . . Delhi Golf Club

1963 DOW FINSTERWALD VS. PETER ALLISS

Jamaica, British Virgin Islands . . . . Tryall

GENE LITTLER VS. ERIC BROWN

Auchterarder, Scotland . . . . Gleneagles

DAVE RAGAN VS. CELESTINO TUPOT

Phillippines . . . . Weck-Weck

ART WALL, JR. VS. STAN LEONARD

Boischatel, Canada . . . . Royal Quebec

DOUG SANDERS VS. ARNE WERKEL

Sweden . . . . Holmsted

JACK NICKLAUS VS. SAM SNEAD

Pebble Beach, California . . . . Pebble Beach

BYRON NELSON VS. GERRY DE WIT

Holland . . . . Hague

PHIL RODGERS VS. FRANK PHILLIPS

Singapore . . . . Royal Singapore

BILLY CASPER VS. HARRY BRADSHAW

Dublin, Ireland . . . . Portmarnock

BOB GOALBY VS. BOB CHARLES

Wellington, New Zealand . . . . Paraparamu Beach

BOB ROSBURG VS. ROBERTO DE VICENZO

Santiago, Chile . . . . Los Leones

1962   JERRY BARBER VS. DAI REES

Surrey, London .... Wentworth

JACK BURKE, JR. VS. STAN LEONARD

Alberta, Canada .... Banff

GENE SARAZEN VS. HENRY COTTON

St. Andrews, Scotland. .... Old Course at St. Andrews

BOB ROSBURG VS. PETE NAKAMURA

Tokyo, Japan .... Kasumigaseld

GENE LITTLER VS. BYRON NELSON

Pine Valley, New Jersey .... Pine Valley

KEN VENTURI VS. UGO GRAPPASONI

Rome, Italy .... Ogliata

GARY PLAYER VS. PETER THOMSON

Melbourne, Australia .... Royal Melbourne

MIKE SOUCHAK VS. ROBERTO DE VICENZO

Buenos Aires, Argentina .... Jockey Club

JAY HEBERT VS. FLORY VAN DONCK

Paris, France...................................... St. Cloud

TED KROLL VS. CHEN CHING PO

Hong Kong .... Royal Hong Kong

BILLY CASPER VS. MARIO GONZALEZ

Rio de Janeiro, Brazil .... Gavea Country Club

INDEX